ABOUT THE A

Richard W H Bray has been in the wine trade since 2001, when he started working for Luvians Bottleshop in Scotland. He was a head sommelier for two years, and has provided independent consultancy and tastings around the world.

In 2008 he flew to France to work his first vintage.

He currently works for an award-winning wine merchant and importer in London. In the evenings and on weekends, he writes. Every year, he returns to the Roussillon to make wine.

RICHARD W H BRAY

SALT
&
OLD
VINES

unbound

2014

THIS EDITION FIRST PUBLISHED IN 2014

UNBOUND

4-7 Manchester Street   Marylebone   London   W1U 2AE
www.unbound.co.uk

Typesetting by Bracketpress
Cover by Mecob
Map illustration ©Gareth Clarke 2013

A CIP record for this book is available
from the British Library

ISBN 978-1-78352-004-6 (trade)
ISBN 978-1-78352-003-9 (ebook)
ISBN 978-1-78352-005-3 (limited edition)

PRINTED AND BOUND IN INDIA BY REPLIKA PRESS PVT. LTD.

For my parents

CONTENTS

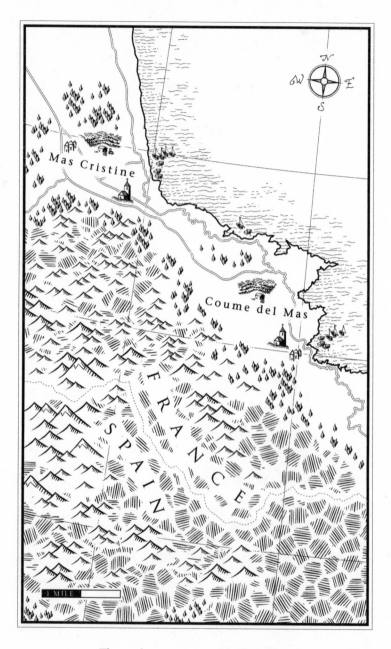

The south-eastern coast of the Roussillon

INTRODUCTION & EXPLANATION

THIS IS THE SECOND BOOK THAT CAME TO ME on a roundabout. The first one is another story, for another time.

This particular roundabout is the one that sits just off the first exit for Argelès and Le Racou after you leave Collioure on the autoroute headed towards Perpignan. It's still in the hilly bit, before the flat bit. We were going the other way; towards Collioure, from Argelès. Andy was driving. He features quite heavily in this book, as it's him that I make wine with. We were heading back towards Collioure from the winery and as we were crossing the roundabout and curling off on the exit towards town, I mentioned that 'some day' I wanted to write a book about wine and this place, that I wanted to call it *Where the Mountains Meet the Sea*. I was telling Andy because he'd mentioned the phrase that I wanted to be the title a few vintages before and I felt that quietly mentioning it without him saying, 'Hey, that's my fucking line' would be his tacit approval of the title. As we took the coast road into Collioure, up and down the hills covered in terraced vines, the sea on our left, and the taller foothills of the Pyrenees rising in front of us to the right, it seemed a good title. At that point that's all it was, just a title and a mention of intent.

It's not even that title anymore.

And 'some day' turned out to be somewhat sooner than I expected.

This isn't a wine book, not really. It has quite a lot of wine in it, both made and drunk. It has some vinous vocabulary, and even a glossary to provide some manner of guide to words like 'remontage' and 'residual sugar'. But the intent is not to teach you everything about wine in the Roussillon, Collioure and Banyuls. It's not a reference guide; I don't even give the addresses of the wineries that I work at (you can probably find them online). Nor is it a collection of tasting notes or maps or diagrams. There are no photos of pristine grapes bathed in the Mediterranean sun. Instead there are stories; the stories about the place and the people that take wine from grape to bottle.

I should also point out that the experiences written here are mine. I don't know of any winery that does things exactly the same as any other winery. The comportes we use hold 50 kilos worth of grapes, the comportes they use in Chablis hold 13 kilos worth. Many wineries don't use comportes; everything just gets bunged into the back of a tractor. Nothing contained in these pages should be considered ubiquitous in the wine world, save perhaps the difficulty of the work and the devotion of those that do it.

While it is a book of stories, it is not without points of reference. Some are scientific, some are historical and some are geographical. I have asked for advice and clarification from several people, though all of the research I've done is my own work. Andy Cook provided the vast bulk of technical knowledge and advice regarding winemaking, but any errors are mine, not his.

– RWHB
June, 2013

MOUNTAINS & WINDOW SEATS

I USED TO GO STRAIGHT FOR AN AISLE SEAT. THE aisle seat meant that, if I had to, I could get up and down without bothering anyone. A good flight was one where I sat down, buckled my seatbelt, pulled my hat over my eyes, fell asleep before take-off and woke to the bump of touch down at our destination. If my eyes did open, I might plug my headphones in and shift a little to get more comfortable; kick my shoes off and make fists with my toes. I'm not chatty on planes, and want them to simply bring me from one place to another. Cocooning myself in sleep, music and maybe a book seemed the best way to do that. Sightseeing could wait until landing.

Perhaps a part of it is growing up. Rightly or wrongly, I viewed the window seat as a feature of an excited childhood. The image of huge tracts of the earth passing in what seems to be slow motion, and in miniature, fires the imagination. Tiny towns, patchwork farmland, mountainous clouds obscuring all of them; more than any other experience of youth, looking out the window of an airplane gives the most incredible glimpse of the wider world around you. It's your first intro-duction to the scale of the earth.

Somewhere along the way, I stopped caring about the scale of the earth. I wore my callousness to it like a badge of honour, and my cocoon on flights made me impervious to whatever might go on in the rest of the world.

In January 2008, after a flight from London to Perpignan, I decided to start sitting in the window seat again. I felt the plane begin its descent, and as our path got steeper and steeper, I kept looking towards the window, over the two people sat next to me. Through the porthole on one side, I saw a plain, dotted with the odd inland sea, stretching out alongside a slate, angry Mediterranean. On the other stood snow-capped mountains, dark forests and the singular peak of what I would later discover was the Canigou, the 9,000 foot mountain sentry that stands guard over the Plaine du Roussillon.

Lone mountains strike a nerve. Whether it's the peak of the Matterhorn, the Paramount Pictures logo or Tolkien's evocative description of Smaug's lair, we feel some sort of deep awe when presented with such natural monuments. Like looking out of an airplane window, they provide a sense of scale.

I nearly gave myself whiplash switching from window to window, trying to see as much as possible.

Flying to the other local airport, Girona, is also rewarding for the window-seat sitter. The flight path takes you down the French side of the Pyrenees, right up until the coast, where the flight banks right, heading west into Spain. The plane's in full descent at this point and the earth seems close, as do the foothills that begin the mountains, rising right out of the sea, stamped on the border like some giant mythical bear paw. If you look closely, between the paw's claws, you'll see the towns of Collioure, Port-Vendres and Banyuls. Closer still, and the vineyard terraces come into focus, with their vines looking for all the world like an ordnance survey map, complete with tightly drawn contour lines.

Within 15 minutes, you've landed in Spain. It's farming

country, and the fields around Girona quite famously smell of pig shit. It's half an hour drive back to the border, and another hour or so to Collioure. Along the way are seedy border towns laden with cheap cigarettes and brothels, including The Dallas in Jonquera, a familiar stop for some of those that work in the vines.

So here we are, lying on the very bottom south-west corner of France. There are no palatial châteaux surrounded by immaculately trained vines (well, there's one, Château Valmy, but compared to those in Bordeaux, it would barely qualify as a gatehouse). Nor are there the gentle slopes and gentrified rusticity of Burgundy, where they had the decency to make their vines accessible to the people that farm them.

Collioure and Banyuls sit near the edge, literally and figuratively. Spain is spitting distance away. Several of the small roads that cross the border bear no notice that you are doing so. As far as landscape goes, it can be difficult to determine where one begins and the other ends. Catalan is spoken on both sides, though less so these days. Legally, this is France, and has been so since the end of the Franco–Spanish War and the Peace of the Pyrenees in 1659. Emotionally, culturally, the people here are Catalan. In the past, they were ruled by both sides and kingdoms that now exist only in history books. They support Barcelona in the football but they play only rugby; union and league. Vines are planted mostly on terraced slopes, though in some places they'll stick them on any spare piece of land. Higher up the hills, there's decay, as the remains of the terraces and drywall slowly rejoin the hillside and the vines give way to scrub and brush. Two of the towns along this stretch of coast, Collioure and Banyuls, also provide the name for the local wine appellations. While they are part of the greater region of the Roussillon, they have been distinguished as warranting a separate classification. Dry table wines from the region are classed as Collioure, whilst fortified sweet wines are classed as Banyuls.

France's appellation system can be labyrinthine, and while it nominally exists to preserve the identity of the thousands of wine-producing regions in the country, it seems mostly to produce endless amounts of paperwork, lab tests, self-sustaining bureaucracy and headaches for winemakers. Their rules range from common sense to the mundane and ulti-mately idiotic. I've never met a winemaker who looks upon their control boards with any sort of fondness or pride (even those that sit on the control boards hold them in a certain measure of disdain). Most importantly, they are boring to write about, read about and talk about. There are numerous wine tomes out there that will help you get a grip with them. This book is not one of them. I shall keep their mention to a minimum.

Vintage begins early in these parts, usually before the end of August. It is one of the earliest harvests in France, and often one of the shortest. It's dry here, and the sun is hot. Too much rain is rarely a problem, though too little frequently can be. The first time I flew here to make wine was August 2008. I had been in the wine trade for eight or so years and when one of my mentors moved from wine merchanting on to wine-making, he invited me over to help out with the harvest.

Just a side note, because sometimes people get confused. Words can be used in perpetuity without a meaning ascribed to them. 'Vintage' is one of those words. People seem to take its meaning as the year a particular wine is made, but that's not the case. Vintage ≠ year. Vintage comes from the French *vendange*, which means harvest. So when you see vintage and then year; that was the year the grapes were harvested. The

[4]

difference isn't huge between the making of a wine and the harvesting of the wine, but there is a difference. As you'll find out through the course of this book, a wine isn't 'made' when the fermentation is finished. There are other steps that take it through the autumn, winter and spring of the new year. It's a long process. Vintage is used because even though the making of the wine can take place over the course of many months (in some cases, with certain wines, over a number of years), much of the character of it is, in most cases, determined by the conditions of the year the grapes were harvested. I will use the term harvest and vintage interchangeably throughout this book. If you already knew this, then this paragraph probably wasn't for you. If you didn't, then you've learned something new. Don't worry, there isn't a test. I've told you to fulfil my own issues with wine pedantry, rather than any mission of enlightenment.

The borders here exist on all levels: physical, national, cultural and geological. The coastal towns sit in natural harbours, bookended by vine-clad cliffs of gnarled schist. The layered stone looks folded, running perpendicular to the earth. The hill peaks are dotted with watchtowers, relics from more war-torn times. Invasion would be signalled from them by the lighting of a bonfire, which would lead to the others following, the flames travelling over the peaks, warning those below of impending conflagration.

Battles these days come on the rugby pitches. While both the French and Spanish sides are Catalan, there are stark differences between the two. The Spanish side is immensely prosperous. It is the industrial and commercial capital of the country whose fortunes were so grand that it enraged Franco, and much of the domestic policy under him was set forth to tip the scales towards the rest of the country.

The French side does not fare as well. It is, in the traditional sense of the word, a peasant region. Small-scale fruit farms and vineyards dot the landscape, while the harbours are filled with small, now-idle, fishing boats. Port-Vendres, sat between Collioure and Banyuls, boasts the deepest harbour in the region, and as such large container ships of fruit from Africa land their produce there, but for the most part everything is on a small scale. Locals farm and fish, or work in Perpignan, the area's largest city that also forms the eastern border of French Catalonia. Then there are the outsiders, those that came for the beauty, the lifestyle by the sea. There are artists and expats, folks from all over France who ran away to find themselves here. Having spent a lot of time in Key West, I see many of the same sort of people – people looking to live on the edge of something. Key West is only 185 miles from Miami, but in many ways, it's as far as you can get from the sense of being in the continental United States while not actually leaving. You're aware that you're closer to Cuba than the mainland, not just geographically, but culturally. Collioure, Banyuls and this little coastal stretch of the Roussillon is as far as you can get from the French and still be in France. Except for during the height of tourist season. Then it's full of French from the rest of the country reminding you constantly that you're definitely in France.

The military is also there, in various shapes and forms. The French marines train in Collioure, whilst there is a not-so-top-secret military base on the Cap Bear peninsula. I've often seen the marines taking their rubber boats out on training exercises, and Collioure is often full of fatigue-garbed French soldiers. I've never seen any vehicle leave or enter the Cap Bear installation.

There are plentiful bars and cafés. A good general rule to

[6]

follow is that the closer they are to the water, the more expensive they will be. That is true whether you're in Collioure, Banyuls, Port-Vendres or Argelès.

I've not mentioned Argelès yet. I should do, but it sits outside the appellation, and so it can't just be lumped in with all the others. This is how my mind works now, for better or for worse; I categorise and organise on the basis of appellation and wine style. Argelès-sur-Mer is the next town to the north of Collioure. It sits at the very beginning of the Plaine du Roussillon. The mountains stop before they get there. The soil changes. The weather is different; not as windy. The changes between places are at once infinitesimal and gargantuan. Argelès is split in two: the old town, which is just Argelès-sur-Mer, and Argelès-Plage, a seaside resort with all the hilarious tackiness that comes with being a seaside resort. Argelès has what I would call a boardwalk area, except that it's an entire village of boardwalks on the beach, with countless t-shirt shops, dodgy fast food stands selling *Americains* (a baguette stuffed with two burgers and generous amounts of chips, usually sprayed liberally with both mayo and ketchup – tremendous hangover food), bad cocktails bars, the odd nightclub, rotating postcard racks, too many tapas bars with bad, low-res photos of what their food is meant to look like, swimwear shops peddling brightly coloured wares; everything is neon, pastel or both. It's a temple to holiday spending. The campsites around the town swell to a population of about 70,000 during the summer – some even have their own water parks.

The older part of town is somewhat more staid. It's in the commuter belt for Perpignan and boasts the usual assortment of bakeries and the like. On the outskirts lives the hypermarché, for when you need to buy Pringles, socks and a 50-inch TV.

The offices and warehouse that we use are located right by the hypermarché as well – it's the industrial neck of town. While most of the restaurants in these parts are the kind of pizza, sandwich, McDonald's sort of dives you'd expect for speedy lunches, there is one corner of the industrial estate that boasts an excellent restaurant run by a chef who trained under all sorts of Michelin-star types and, for some reason, decided, when searching for his own corner of the restaurant world, to open up on an industrial estate in Argelès-sur-Mer. I either can't remember the name or want to keep the place a secret so that it doesn't get too busy. It may be a mixture of the two.

The wines from Argelès belong to the Côtes du Roussillon appellation. This is the largest AOC (Appellation d'Origine Contrôlée) in the region. I make wines here, at Mas Cristine, as well as in the Collioure appellation, at Coume del Mas (though that winery actually sits between Banyuls and Port-Vendres, and the grapes come mostly from around Banyuls).

Going from east to west (and north to south along the coastline), it's Argelès, Collioure, Port-Vendres, Banyuls and Cerbère. I will most likely never write about or mention Cerbère again as it is an utter shithole and the most interesting thing I can think of to say about it is that we once blew out a tyre there on the drive back from Spain. We'd gone to Spain for lunch, because we can do that in this neck of the woods, and had one of the truly worst lunches I have ever willingly eaten. Ever. Blowing out the tyre was better than the lunch. I don't think anyone present that afternoon would disagree with me. I once saw an article recommending Cerbère as a good place to go in France as its beaches were always empty, even in August. There's a good reason for it to be empty, even in August; it's not a very nice place.

Harvest moves from south to north. It starts in the vines around Banyuls first, with those around Collioure following about a week later, and Argelès another week after that. From there it spreads both east and north, moving as the vines and the grapes on them reach their full ripeness. Why does it move that way? Temperature and sunlight, mostly. The berries form in the late spring. By July, veraison begins to set, where the fruit reaches its full size. From there forth, the grapes ripen. Sunlight feeds the leaves, which put most of their energy towards making sure the berries are packed with as much sugar as possible. Sunlight = sugar. People talk about warm temperatures all the time, but heat and haze makes things difficult. The result on the growing season is remarkable. We discovered in one year that heat without direct sunlight can be disastrous. Bunches do not ripen evenly, with some grapes being laden with sugar and others barely registering on the refractometer. You want to make wine with evenly ripened bunches.

At Coume del Mas, the winery near Banyuls, we start checking the bunches in early August. It's a simple process. You wander around the vineyard with a wee ziplock sandwich bag, picking grapes from a random selection of vines spread out across as much of the plot as possible. Then you scrunch the grapes in the bag, crushing them and smooshing them until it's all a big wet, gooey mess. Then you pour the juice onto the end of the refractometer, a nifty little cylinder that looks like a weird telescope or kaleidoscope. You hold your eye to the non-juiced end and the light passing through the grape juice bounces differently according to the level of sugar. This is important, as the amount of sugar translates directly as the amount of potential alcohol you can expect from the finished wine. Boozy spyglasses are one of the many fine toys you get to play with as a winemaker.

[9]

So that's it, right? If there's loads of sugar in the grapes, they're ready to pick, obviously. Not so fast, boozy mcbooze-hound. Sugar is all well and good, but if that were the only important thing we'd all be wrecked on cachaça. For every grape you put in your ziplock baggie, you also pop one in your mouth. Boozy spyglasses are all well and good, but while they can tell you how much sugar is in something they can't tell you anything else. They can't tell you how acidic the grapes are. Nor do they whisper in your ear the texture of the grape skins. And most importantly, they don't tell you how they all work together, how the acidity balances the sugar and how the texture of the skins grips your mouth. Tasting grapes is a serious business, and while sugar levels give you a literal translation of ripeness, it tells you nothing of harmony and balance within the fruit.

Plenty of wineries pick entirely based on sugar ripeness. I've met some high level winemakers who see no reason to do otherwise, but we use it to provide a rough window. With dozens of different vineyards to pick, scattered over much of the region, our decision is down to taste. There are some very wealthy wineries that do a full analysis of particular phenols (anthocyanins and tannins) to determine picking time. I'm told it's a big thing in Bordeaux.

Vineyard holdings down here are piecemeal. The idea of long stretches of unbroken plots of singularly owned vines is nice, but not applicable in these parts. The terraced vineyards that dot the hillside display a patchwork of different owner-ships. Each bit of patchwork with its own wee *casot*: a small shed for storing water and equipment, looking too much like a beach hut out of place. I don't think any of our vines sit next to any of our other vines. If they do, they're in the minority. The vines around Banyuls stretch right into frontier land, outside of civilisation. Wild forests, cork forests, armies of wild boar (*sangliers* in the local parlance), ancient, decaying farmhouses and the occasional hippy are all that you're likely to see in these parts. The roads that bring you are one lane, and rarely paved. The stream beds are dry, as they are for most of the season. They run freely in the spring, swollen and fast. But now, in harvest, their beds are raw with stone and dust. These valleys trap the sun, and in the heat the vivid green of the foliage hangs in stark contrast to the arid schist soils that hold the vines.

And what is schist? Schist is old rock formed from older clay. The name's evocative, onomatopoeic. It suggests shards in my mind and lo, that is what you see all around as you wander the vineyards, shards of rock, sometimes terribly brittle. Often the rock looks as though someone's kicked up the edge of a carpet. Good wine grows on schist soils, some far more famous than the ones here. The Douro Valley, renowned for Port, boasts schist soils, as does the Spanish region of Priorat. Both regions feature rough terrain and precarious terraces on which their vines are planted. Both Port and Banyuls produce profound fortified wines whilst both Priorat and Banyuls make great, dry Grenache-based wines. One of my favourite wines is named Schistes, in honour of the soil from which it comes, and shapes its character in ways that we still don't entirely understand.

It used to be thought that certain soil characteristics were directly passed from root, to vine, to berry, to wine. There are still some that cling to this, though scientific study disproves it almost entirely. A Chablis may taste chalky, and the soil it comes from may be composed of mostly chalk, but chemically speaking, there is no chalk in the wine to speak of. The research is conclusive in that regard, but it leaves more questions unanswered than answered, as much good science does. In my head, the soil's impact on good wine is much like a sculptor's chisel. The finished sculpture bears no obvious mark of the chisel, but its effect is evident throughout.

I have no research to back this up but thousands of wines tasted, and the anecdotal measure of my palate.

When I arrive for vintage, I fly into Girona, a small town in Spain about an hour's drive from Barcelona. Andy, my old friend/former boss/mentor picks me up from the airport and we catch up along the way. I'm tired from travel but giddy with the sunshine. The car smells a bit of sulphur and farm gear. The stereo pumps out one of his mix CDs and he brings me up to speed on the harvest so far: what's been picked, what's next to be picked, how big it's looking and where I'll be staying.

Andy Cook was my first boss in the wine trade, the manager of a small shop in St Andrews called Luvians Bottleshop. He taught me about wine and taught me to teach myself about wine. He started as a sommelier at the age of 17 and from then on had sold wine, bought wine, made wine and drunk quite a lot of it as well. After ten years running the wine shop in Scotland, he moved to New Zealand to learn both viticulture and winemaking at a higher level. He then moved to France with his (now) wife Kirsten to work with Philippe Gard at Mas Cristine and Coume del Mas, taking head winemaker duties at Mas Cristine and running most of the sales for both wineries.

Our shared history is one of too much whisky, the occasional sevens rugby tournament, too much beer, lots of blues music, the occasional AC/DC air guitar session, bankrupting fine dining dinners, too much wine, boozy milkshakes, beach frisbee, too many Brandy Alexanders and hard work. Andy has remarkable impatience for most things except wine, though his two young boys, Theo and Angus, have forced him to count longer than five before he loses his temper. Andy works harder than anyone I know, and expects others to do the same. He won't tell anyone to do anything he hasn't done himself or isn't willing to do himself. I'm reflexively lazy. My work ethic, if you can call it that, is based on the fear of being discovered to be as lazy as I actually am. It's why I work well with Andy, and now Philippe as well. They work so hard that if I don't, it becomes very apparent very quickly. I would really rather be sleeping until 2 p.m. and drinking peanut butter and bourbon milkshakes in my pyjamas while watching *Mythbusters* on Netflix. But I can't, so I bust my ass with them in a winery. Two wineries.

So, born out of my fear of getting caught napping, I've become a member of this team, helping my friend make wine.

That team changes from year to year, with the *stagaires* – interns from oenology school, usually Toulouse or Bordeaux – and the *vendangeurs* – migrant pickers from as close as Spain and as far afield as French Polynesia – rarely coming back. The core remains the same: Philippe, resident genius, director, winemaker, viticulturalist, geological expert and head honcho; Julien, the vine grower and Catalan native who knows literally everybody, has played rugby with them and who they all undoubtedly owe a favour; José, the retired Spanish banker who now 'runs the vines', which is a lot more difficult than it sounds, and the senior picking team, including Vincent, José's son, the improbably named Igor and the grumpy dude with a goatee who thinks I'm crazy for coming back every year. His name's Stephane. He thinks I'm an idiot. Which is probably true.

We drive straight to the winery. Time is limited at harvest, and unpacking and getting settled are luxuries not afforded to anyone. I've learned this and have my boots and work clothes right at the top of my bag. I find a private corner of the cave and slip into my tattered shorts, stained t-shirt and a battered pair of hiking boots that, at this point, can be used for nothing but winemaking. This is my uniform for the next month or so. I will maybe have three days in 35 that I don't don some variation of this kit and get very, very messy.

The village of Cosprons sits between Banyuls and Port-Vendres. It is famous for artisan Banyuls vinegar and the ruins of one of Alfred Nobel's first dynamite factories. A dry river bed runs next to the village, so long barren that rows of Mourvèdre vines now grow where the water used to flow Vines rise up the banks as well, some terraced and some slopes gentle enough not to require it. Many of these vines were irreparably damaged, not by hail, but by Andy's old labrador, Alfie, careening through them to fetch sticks we threw to keep him occupied. Just before you get to Cosprons, coming from the main road, is a small dirt track descending down towards the river bed. There is a battered white wooden sign that marks the road, saying simply 'caves'. *Caves* is French for caves, but also for winery. This particular winery is Coume del Mas, though there is nothing to indicate that this is the case. There's no sign above the large barn doors. There's no street number. I'm not even sure the dirt track has a name.

The building is large and simple, with a sloped roof and concrete floor angled downwards that allows liquid, be it wine, water or whatever, to drain into a narrow central gutter. The two large wooden doors open inward, revealing an open-plan winery with a cool room in the back. That's where the barrels of white live. Above the cool room, in the attic, lay barrels of fortified wine, ageing in the warmest part of the winery. Some of these will become 'Rancio' style Banyuls and some 'Grand Cru'. To the left of the main floor sit five large stainless steel fermentation tanks, shiny, numbered 1 to 5. To the right is a massive, 4,000 litre ancient oak *foudre* (a barrel too large to be called a barrel anymore) and next to that is a 5,000 litre brand new oak fermentation vat. In front of the *foudre* is a glass display shelf, with dummy bottles from old vintages, a few tasting glasses and a nice wine thief. A wine thief is a large pipette used to take samples of wine from a barrel. In the back is a ratty-looking plastic wine thief – that's what I use when I have to get samples out. The customers get the pretty wine thief.

The view from the cave is stunning: the old river valley below and ahead, nestled between two cliffs, the Mediterranean spreads out into the horizon. Early mornings made far more bearable by the ghostly dawn that grows over the sea until a tangerine sun rises from the deep blue. Everything goes quiet for the sunrise, even though the work doesn't stop.

We make a bunch of different wines: red, white, rosé, sweet, dry, fortified, unfortified. Most of our wines fall within the local classifications as either Collioure (dry) or Banyuls (sweet; fortified). Then there are some weird and wonderful cuvées that don't necessarily fit within the narrow confines of appellation law. These tend to be small batches from small parcels of grapes that show something a little bit special. Maybe they've ripened slower and need a bit more time on the vines; or perhaps they're from a particularly old group of vines; maybe something has happened during ferment to mark them as a breed apart; regardless, they warrant a separation.

We meet in the dark, in an old parking lot in the centre of Banyuls. There are maybe 20 of us in total, winemakers and pickers. It's mostly pickers. Nobody is awake yet, bar Philippe, the founder of Coume del Mas, who apparently needs far less time to achieve full consciousness than the rest of us. There's no list of the top winemakers in the south of France that doesn't include him. You wouldn't know it to look at him. He's diminutive, with a mop of dark hair that seems to accent the look of constant problem-solving on his face. There's not much written down at the winery. There's no rule book or game plan or even floor plan. It's all in his head. I've never seen him puzzle too long over a decision. He gets through vintages with the same wounds, scrapes and bruises the rest of us do, and yet he keeps going. One year, while moving the sorting table on to the back of the truck to bring it through from Coume del Mas to Mas Cristine, it dislodged and hit him in the head. Another inch or so and it would have killed him. Instead, it concussed him and left a nasty gash in his skull. He was back in the winery the next day, much to the annoyance of both his doctor and his wife, Nathalie.

One particularly brutal vintage, about four weeks in, my right arm went dead. I could no longer lift from the elbow. I had never had muscle fatigue before. My fingers still worked, so I could grip things tight. It was an enormous harvest that year. I probably lifted about six or so tons of grapes a day, plus the other muscle-intensive tasks. I cheated to my left as much as I could and it got to the point where I dreaded using my right arm. When I did have to use that arm to shift weight, usually a comporte, up above my chest, I did it with my legs and back, using my grip to guide it. It was dangerous. One afternoon when the Mourvèdre was coming in, Philippe and I started unloading the truck and I cheated to my left. He stopped and signalled to his right arm, shook his head and made the 'cut' sign across his neck with his left hand. It wasn't just me. We both had dead arm. Philippe cheated to his left and I somehow managed on the right.

That moment sticks with me. Everybody hurts during harvest, even the boss; especially the boss.

That same year, right at the beginning of harvest, I had an accident with the liquid CO_2, which is quite the most rubbish liquid to have an accident with. I was gassing a tank of Roussanne at Mas Cristine before sealing it up for the end of the day and the handle slipped. I was on top of the ladder and the gas tank stood to my right. The only way to not lose balance or knock over the tank (which, being a highly compressed gas, could explode, both killing me and, worse, ruin all the whites in the chill container) was to grab the tank with my free hand and somehow keep grip on the nozzle whose handle had broken. This involved grabbing a metal joint at the end of the hose. One that, it turned out, had a bit of a leak, and was frosted over with the remnants of the liquid CO_2. The webbing between my thumb and forefinger froze tight to the metal joint. It stung like a motherfucker. I could feel the cold burning through the skin down to the muscle. Still off-balance, I tried to drop the nozzle and hose to the ground, and hope that it didn't upend the gas cylinder, but that joint on the hose was now just stuck to my hand. So I tore it off, expecting a massive chunk of my hand to come off with it.

The cylinder didn't upend, and the ladder held. My hand felt very hot and very cold at the same time. I got the hat on the tank of Roussanne and sealed it. I then put the ladder away in the corner. Then I realised the gas was still on, and using my good hand, I turned it off and gently shimmied the tank to its spot in the gap between the two large tanks in the centre of the container. I looked over the container a few more times to make sure that everything was put away. By the door sat a red comporte full of water and SO_2, used for quickly cleaning bits of kit and flushing through the pumps and hoses when they're finished for the day. I still couldn't look at it, but I put my left hand in the comporte and sucked in air as it met with the mix of water and sulphur. It hurt. I lifted it out of the water and looked at the spot where the metal had frozen itself to me (it was the metal's fault entirely). There was no gaping wound, no hole in my hand. Instead rose an enormous blister; it grew so quickly that within a minute or two I couldn't close my hand properly. I couldn't work with only one hand, so I lanced it. It went deep, through the skin to the flesh. Within a day's work, it had torn off completely and for the rest of harvest the burn was exposed. There was nothing I could do. The work was too wet to dress it properly. To this day, I have what looks like a cigar burn on the webbing of that hand, though it's faded somewhat now. After a few days I didn't really notice it while I worked. It was only when I tried to sleep that it burned.

Philippe lays out the day for us in that parking lot. We're told where we need to be. It's all in French and my stunted linguistic abilities leave me searching for some sort of signal. I usually know, though, that I'm going to the winery. The pickers are going to the vines, often with Philippe going with them.

The pickers are a mix of known and unknown. The locals run the crew. They're young and still look on me like some sort of alien. I don't envy their task. The migrant pickers are a cocktail mix of hippies and hipsters. Some come from Spain, some from elsewhere entirely. We've had the odd Brit on gap year, but they never last long. The chasm between the romantic ideal of working in the vines and the reality of working in the vines has no gentle bridge for them to cross, and so usually they get sent packing. The hipsters and hippies seem a bit better suited for the work. They need the money, so they do the work. They don't know much about wine, but that's no problem. They bust their humps from the early hours of the morning to the late afternoon and then go home with some unlabelled co-op wine we keep just to reward their hard work.

The first grapes picked are white. We pick them before the pickers arrive. It's a family affair, with Philippe and his wife, Nathalie, taking their girls up to the Roussanne vineyard that sits high in the hills above Banyuls. Roussanne tends to ripen early in these parts. It's a white grape made famous in the Northern Rhône, gaining popularity among those who like big whites but with perfume and a bit of spice. We grow it in both appellations. These grapes get blended with Vermentino to make one of our smallest cuvées. It's for local customers only, though on occasion it travels as far as Toulouse.

This small family ritual heralds the harvest. I've never arrived early enough for it, but there's no shame in that. Vintage is long and family time is scarce in the meantime. To welcome it with family is a good thing. The cuvée label bears the names of the family members who pick the grapes. Even though I don't pick the grapes, I always smile when I analyse the barrel. Every year, regardless of the harvest conditions, those vessels of fermenting grape juice mark the beginning of a new year. No matter what order everything else comes in, those are the first. And when so much relies on the weather, and the fickle ripening habits of grape, it's nice to have at least one thing you can count on to be constant, year in and year out.

There are only 13 independent wine producers in Collioure and Banyuls, an area that covers 1540 hectares of vine. It's quite small by most standards. A hectare, by the way, works out at about 2.2 acres, and is essentially 100 metres by 100 metres. The more vines you plant per hectare, the more wine you get (in theory). The problem, round these parts, is that the hectares aren't flat. They're steep. It's also incredibly dry, so the vines are subjected to what we call water stress. Meaning that they're stressed that they can't get very much water. This has huge effect on the wine. Less water means more concentrated grapes, but it can also prevent the fruit from developing properly. And, of course, irrigation for viticulture is illegal for appellation wines in France. Fortifying wine originated in these parts, for good reason, as wine made from very ripe grapes could be inherently unstable, due to high sugar levels leading to re-fermentation.

Most 1540 hectares worth of vines would boast a lot more than 13 independent vignerons. Throughout the rest of France, it may be as many as ten times that number. Those 13 independent vignerons (ourselves included) account for only 15% of the production. The rest of it goes through the enormous co-operative in Banyuls. Co-ops are just what they sound like – consortiums of grape growers that group together their individual parcels of grapes, split costs and share revenues. If it sounds like a socialist ideal, that's because it is. Except for the attempts to make profits. That isn't terribly socialist. The hideous state of management and internal bickering is, however, and is enough to make a Fox News anchor drool. I should say that there are plenty of brilliantly run co-ops throughout France, because there are. They make great wine and provide a living for the growers that supply them. The level of quality considering the enormous quantity is admirable, and requires truly brilliant winemaking. There are even those elsewhere in the Roussillon that manage to make good wine, reward their growers and turn a profit. But the cave co-op in Banyuls, in spite of making some great wine, doesn't seem able to reward its growers or turn a profit. And the one in Argelès, in spite of being reasonably well-run, makes truly dreadful wine.

Morning starts at Coume del Mas before sunrise. The winery door opens to the dry river bed lined with vines and the sea in the distance. We move slow, but with purpose. Sometimes the truck is sat outside, waiting with grapes in its refrigerated container. If it is, we set up quickly.

If the grapes are white, we get the press ready. A press is a giant cylinder with a bag in it. Well, our press is. It's called a bag press. The grapes go into the cylinder and then we inflate the bag. Half the cylinder is grated, allowing the juice to pour through it as the bag inflates. The juice pours into a tray attached below the cylinder, and then pumped from that tray into an old milk tank to settle over night. The first time I saw a press, so much dawned on me. As a piece of kit, it's a great reminder that all you're dealing with is grape juice. The grapes get squeezed, their juice comes out, you put that juice into a tank and then it ferments and becomes wine. I knew that on an intellectual level, obviously. But there's a big gap between the knowledge of something at an intellectual level and truly understanding; truly 'getting' it; to be watching torrents of sugar water drip off stainless steel and knowing that that's what you're working for. That's your raw material to make wine. The continuing work of years and the immediate work of the last ten or so months, vineyard management and pruning and pulling out weeds and ploughing, all of that for a steady stream of juice dripping into a big plastic tray. It's remarkable and simple all at once.

The grapes are transported and stored in comportes. A comporte is the modern version of a peasant's wicker harvest basket. Sometimes they're called bins – *comporte* is the French term for them. They're made of plastic, hold about 50 kilograms worth of grape bunches, and are designed to fit together like a child's building blocks, so that they can be stacked atop each other safely. Sort of like giant, grape-bearing Lego. There are two types that I've come across: red comportes and fucking bastard comportes. Red comportes are moulded from a single piece of plastic, are watertight so that you don't lose any juice, and have rounded handles that provide comfort to whoever has to lift it.

Fucking bastard comportes are yellow, brown or grey. They're prone to snapping in odd areas. Odd areas like the handles, so that they can slice and pinch the webbing between your thumb and forefinger. There are plenty of holes for grape juice to piss out all over the poor bugger dumping its contents into the press or de-stemmer. Their handles are squared, ensuring that they cut deep into the hands when carrying any weight over two or three kilos. I'm quite sure that fucking bastard comportes were designed by a vengeful teetotaller whose heart was broken by someone unloading grapes off the back of a refrigerated lorry.

You should not lift a comporte on your own. You frequently have to, but always try to find someone to help first. Standard practice is one person on each side, each holding a handle. You then count to three and lift as one. The first comporte is the easiest, as you aren't sticky and slippery yet.

CRICKET & LUNCH BREAKS

WE ONLY HARVEST GRAPES WHEN THEY'RE properly ripe. Grapes that are properly ripe are juicy and bursting with sugary goodness. It's important that this is the case, because without that sugar there will be no booze, and without that booze we're wasting a lot of time and energy making smoothies. Supermarket fruit and veg aisles may have dulled most folks to what proper ripe fruit is, when it's grown properly. Ripe fruit explodes. Ripe grapes burst from within like nothing you've ever seen. Their innards are sticky, viscous, globular fleshy lumps of what is essentially one of nature's very own candies. As they are nature's very own candies, the entirety of nature seems to want to munch on them. In the vines they bring down wild boar from the hills, who have destroyed whole tracts of our Syrah vines. In fact, the boar are so fond of the Syrah that we've actually named a Syrah after them.

I avoid picking grapes at every opportunity. I'm not good at it and seem incapable of improving. So I try to avoid it. But sometimes I can't. You do what you're told at vintage, and sometimes you're told to pick grapes.

We meet in the morning, in a parking lot above Collioure, on the roundabout by the cemetery. Already, pastel pinks and blues spread amongst the twilight grey sky. An older Audi pulls up and from it a tall, white-haired man with wire specs and a battered white polo shirt emerges. His clothes hang loose and his hair is thinning but still mane-like. Andy introduces us and his handshake is firm. His name is Yves, he's a retired journalist who owns some vines, though not the ones we're picking today.

Philippe arrives with the truck and we follow him up to Le Rimbau, the high hills behind the town. The valleys form natural amphitheatres; terraced with vines, criss-crossed with lanes, paths, roads and dry-stone gutters. Cork oak forests border the vines giving home to countless wild boar.

We park at the top of the Catala vineyard and the rest of the pickers arrive. Pickers come in all shapes and sizes. Some are Gallic caricatures: thin, goateed and with a rolled cigarette hanging permanently from the corner of their mouths. One year, there was a South Pacific rugby player; mountainous, earning extra cash between weekly matches. Some work in the vines all year round, others are *vendangeurs*, here just for the season. They live on campsites or in cheap flats, drink wine, smoke dope and, hopefully, work hard.

Everyone grabs a bucket and a pair of secateurs. The vineyard is cone-shaped, wide at the top and then tapering down to a narrow point at the bottom of the hill. It faces south/south-east, getting as much sun as possible. The upper half is properly terraced with drywall, while the lower plantings sit untamed on the slope. The vines are Grenache Gris, and their bunches are ripe and dark. Some of the vines have been shaped by the wind and lean awkwardly away from the source of the gales.

Philippe tells me not to pick anything ridden with rot, while Andy warns me away from 'second set'. Second set are bunches that develop later and higher up the vine. They look perfect; tiny bunches that rarely bear any blemishes of the season. They're easier to find and to pick and never have any bugs crawling through them. They appear as an idealised aesthetic concept of a bunch of wine grapes. So of course you can't pick them. They're under ripe. It's the enormous bunches, bursting with ripe fruit and grown so large some need two hands to guide into the bucket, with the odd berry blemish and the occasional smooshed grape, the ones hidden under a thicket of leaves, twisted between two branches of vine, clutched by the small green tendrils of vine creep, whose stems are obscured by the sheer mass of fruit ripened by a summer of the Mediterranean sun, those are the ones that need to be picked. When it's Grenache of any tint, there's a whiff of honeysuckle accompanying the bunches as they drop into the bucket.

The slope is steep; precarious, and it gets steeper as we work down the vines. We pick as we descend and as we get further down we reach the rows that cannot be ploughed, even by horse. On either side the underbrush encroaches.

Once we reach the bottom we about-face and pick on ascent. The schist terrain is loose, bordering on unstable. Rocks like shards slip under foot and the pickers' feet start many a mini avalanche.

Old Grenache vines, Noir, Gris or Blanc, begin to look more and more like the wrong side is buried. They twist and tangle, looking like a hydra or the Kracken. Gnarled and knotted, the strong Mediterranean sun bleaches the bark and, were it not for the luminous green of the dinner-plate sized leaves, you would think they were dead. The canopies are large, important to protect the grapes from that beating sun. However, the leaves combined with the labyrinthine branches make picking the bunches somewhat less straightforward than those of those tidy trellised rows that appear in all the pictures. The vines don't grow tall, they grow out; they spread their tendrils as wide as can be. To the uninitiated it can be a tricky business. You're snipping blind. Secateurs happen to be very sharp. It's very easy to slice a finger and not realise it until you see the blood falling on the schist.

The pickers joke and smoke and grumble and make great pace ascending the vineyard. Aside from rolling or lighting their smokes they don't stop for anything. Once their buckets are full, they empty them into the porteur's tub.

The porteur's job is unenviable. Strapped to his back sits a conical white plastic tub that can hold over 50 kilograms of grapes. The tub has curved lips on either side, so that when the porteur empties it, he just tips sideways towards a waiting comporte. He steps precariously from picker to picker, and then up through the rows of vines, back to the trucks and comportes. The mini avalanches that perturb the pickers pose more of a threat to the porteur. You wouldn't know it to watch him, imperturbable, the shards of schist slipping down the slope beneath his feet. Just a brief pause to collect himself and up he climbs. He's in constant motion and needs to work even quicker than the pickers. No one wants to wait on the porteur.

As the sun rises higher towards noon, so too do we as we pick vine after vine. The heat creeps up on you as the morning fades. I realise too late that I didn't drink any water before we left the house and the drums start in my temples. Standing up from each vine thrusts a blade into my head and I need a second or two to get my bearings. Halfway back up the vines I drop a rotten bunch onto the ground and the head picker starts swearing. He chats to Andy and Andy chats to me. I'm dropping too much fruit. Being too picky.

And I learned an important lesson: fruit isn't perfect, and seeking perfect fruit is a luxury that few wineries can afford. Vineyards are not the fresh produce section of a supermarket. My idea of grapes and the reality was somewhat disjointed. A bunch of healthy grapes with a section suffering from rot? Pull the rotted bit off and keep going.

Suitably chastised, I do keep going, but ever slower. My head is now in constant pain with dehydration and the giggles of the other growers begin to prey on my confidence. I feel their eyes, and in my imagination my incompetence grows with every bunch that falls into my bucket. In my mind, they laugh at my slowness. In reality, they laugh at my presence. They cannot believe that I am here willingly, on my holiday. The idea that their brutal work is something people would pursue as some sort of perverse recreation is hilarious to them. Understandably so, I suppose.

We reach the top and the last porteur tub tips into a comporte and we decamp to the next vineyard. It is tiny, well under a hectare, twice as steep as Catala and incredibly narrow. This is Consolation, just by the L'ermitage de Notre Dame de Consolation. A tiny sliver of steep ground, sparsely planted mostly with Grenache Gris. The base of the vineyard is also the base of the valley, a seeming subtropical forest of odd undergrowth hugging the banks of the stream that runs only when the rains fall.

I've lost interest in keeping pace and my speed is determined only by how much pain my head can take as we go. None of the other pickers have slowed, or even seem terribly tired. It's afternoon now and the sun is beating down. I leap over a small gully and bend down to start on a vine when someone shouts at me. Another important lesson learned. Not all the vineyards are separated by something so obvious as drywall, and the small drainage gully I leapt over turned out to be a property marker as well. Picking other people's vines is frowned upon, because it is stealing and it's not rocket science to work out who's responsible. These are cash crops, and growers make little enough for their work as it is.

Once again chastised, I move on and find a vine with peculiar grapes. They're red wine coloured, with the translucency of an aged Burgundy. This confuses me as grapes don't tend to be the colour of the wine they produce, whether it's red or white. Andy has no idea what they are. The bunches are long and the berries are big. They look like eating grapes. We pick them anyway. They turned out to be a rare variety called San Sebastien.

We're finished by 14.30. The pickers climb onto the back of the truck and from nowhere a box of wine appears, joints are sparked and the engine fires up. They disappear down the dirt road towards town leaving a cloud of dust and echoes of laughter to mark their presence. I hobble towards the car, my legs battered, head pounding and hands bleeding in various places. As I collapse into the passenger seat, Andy asks how I liked picking.

'I think I prefer working in the winery.'

At the winery, processing grapes brings its own menagerie. Wasps, hornets, earwigs, spiders, daddy longlegs and strange white/translucent arachnids all seek the grapes' nectar or, in the spiders' case, those seeking the nectar. Winemakers are not immune to arachnophobia, and I've yet to meet someone not a little unnerved by a three inch hornet, so there is the odd bit of flailing and freaking out whilst shifting comportes.

So as we shift these great plastic baskets of explodingly ripe grapes, our grip gets steadily worse, slicked with must. Must gets everywhere. Grape innards get everywhere. You bend down and look at your loading partner, waiting for the nod to lift and upturn. It's important to nod, to know what the other is doing, as by this point the trailer is slick and dangerous. You press down on your feet, to make sure they won't slip. And then you lift and tip, upending comporte after comporte into the press. After a while, it's the momentum alone that keeps you going. If it's fucking bastard comportes, your fingers begin to lock in shape – it's best to leave them like that until the truck is empty.

As the press fills, you need to take breaks and spread the grapes evenly in the cylinder, to fit as many per pressing as possible. At Coume del Mas, we press in small batches – 18–20 comportes per pressing. At Mas Cristine, it's a bigger press, and we'll try to get as many as 40 comportes in. So 2,000 kilos of grapes. We'll run the press three times a day when all the whites are coming in. So that's 6,000 kilos, loaded by hand, before the day is done.

Once the press is full, we slam the door shut and make sure everything's in place. Then we plug it in. You never fill the press when it's plugged in. It's not so much that there's a risk of you falling in and the bag inflating and pressing you in with the grape juice, though that is indeed the stuff of nightmares. It's more the relentlessness of something as simple as rotating the cylinder. It could snap off a limb and shatter bone. And so it sits unplugged while we fill it.

We set some manner of programme and it twirls around, the grate facing down and a wash of free-run juice pours forth. This is the liquid that needs no coaxing, only gravity, that comes from the weight of the grapes upon themselves and their own vitality, that they were already at bursting point and just needed a little push to share. Press programmes work in stages, starting at lower atmospheric pressures and gradually increasing over the course of a few hours. The juice from the lower pressures is the purest; the fruitiest; the sweetest. As the pressure increases and the liquid left over decreases, the contact with the skins and stems and pips leads to more phenolic juice. We call them secondary flavours. You don't want too much late press juice. Have you ever chewed on a stick? The last presses are basically squeezing juice out of sticks. We taste at every phase to make sure the juice is still balanced and tastes in no way of sticks. When it starts to taste of sticks, we switch tanks, and save what's called the 'press juice' separately. The sound of hydraulics and pumps hammers around and then there is the shriek as the bag deflates.

The press is thorough. It rolls around, allowing the fruit to distribute evenly, and then the bag slowly inflates, squeezing the berries against the walls, their juices pouring forth. The bag then deflates and once again the cylinder rotates, mixing the pulverised berries around before it stops and the bag starts to fill again, this time at a higher pressure.

As the press does its job, we do ours. Comportes need to be cleaned before they go back into the truck for more grapes, so while the press works, we use a pressure hose to rinse all the skins and bugs and must off of the plastic baskets. Grape must left untended in the sunshine can be dangerous. It can start to ferment or oxidise and contaminate or infect new grapes coming in or even affect other juice pre-ferment. It's not guaranteed to happen, in fact it's a longshot, but the chances of it happening become a lot higher if you don't practice good hygiene. I'm probably going to mention this a lot, but much of winemaking is cumulative; it's about good practice and repetition. If you have great soils, climate, vines and fruit, most of your job is done for you (by done for you, I mean that you have to spend every day taking care of your vines to make sure that both they and the fruit they bear are great).

Intervention with the wine should be kept to a minimum. But intervention can come from man or microbes, and to prevent the latter everything has to be kept clean. Grape detritus gets everywhere and must be cleaned away. It's not quite operating theatre level of clean, but it's a close as we can get under the circumstances.

As the tray beneath the press fills with juice, we hit the pump and it sucks the liquid through and into a tank. All the whites go into tank first, even those that will eventually go into barrel for their fermentation. They stay in tank for a day or two, which allows the solids, or lees, to settle to the bottom, leaving remarkably clear juice. Gravity is incredible.

Wine hoses are plastic reinforced with coiled metal, and the valves at either end are stainless steel. The standard size that we use has the diameter of a clenched fist. We fasten the hoses to the lips of the tanks with a supply of tattered bungee cords whose elasticity has all but faded. A badly secured hose loses wine. A hose valve without the small rubber washer to seal it loses wine (extra rubber washers are stored in almost every available space in case of emergency). Losing wine is the ultimate sin. Personal injury, though discouraged, is preferable to losing wine. Everything bar a broken bone or the loss of a limb should be sacrificed for the sake of grapes and wine.

While I'm talking about personal safety, it's important to remind those beginning to get romantic thoughts about winemaking that there is nothing cuddly in a winery. The materials are steel, oak, hardened plastic, epoxy and sometimes concrete. The edges are sharp and hard. Something as simple as the steel end of a hose banging against your shin can wind you with the pain. Quite a lot of the work is done at the top of a precariously stationed ladder. Your safety is very much your responsibility. If you hurt yourself, make sure it isn't serious. If it is, tell someone, if it isn't, shut up and deal with the pain. Because everyone is hurt. Everyone got their fingers caught between loaded comportes, or pulled something trying to lift something, or smacked their knee on the metal end of a hose. Everyone is bruised somewhere and bleeding somewhere. No one got enough sleep and the coffee is utterly revolting. The taste wakes you up more than the caffeine does.

Pumps are a pain. Frequently you flip the switch and the direction is wrong, pumping air into the wine you're supposed to be pulling through. At Coume del Mas, there's a set of power plugs that somehow inverts the default direction of everything that gets plugged into them. So the grape escalator (which is exactly what it sounds like) goes down instead of up, and you have to be savvy when using the pump as the plug turns it all into opposite day. I'm not sure why this happens. I'm not sure why it's never been fixed. It's become one of those things you forget to tell the newbie, and then have to rush to hit the big red emergency stop button on whatever piece of equipment is moving backwards. Everything electrical in a winery has a big red emergency stop button.

The grapes define the day. You work until most are processed – you never want to leave too many in cold storage overnight. Ideally, none at all.

Lunch comes when it can. Sometimes it's early, sometimes it's late. The pickers have to eat, as do the winemakers, though the pickers tend to eat first. The winemakers process the pickers' last load at the winery and then, if all's going well, the winemakers overturn comportes, making them into stools and a lunch table, and out comes bread and cheese and wine and pâté and water and saucisson and salad. We rinse the

[32]

wineglasses with the pressure hose and pour glasses for every-one. Nobody drinks too much wine. A glass or two. I always try to drink as much water as I can. We sit and talk about the grapes coming in later that afternoon, or how the ferments are going. At Coume del Mas there's a local guy who brings us his homemade sausage made from pig's head. Don't flinch; it's delicious (though I'll admit, I flinched at first). Philippe has family in Roquefort country, and one year, towards the end of vintage, he brought down some artisan Roquefort cheese, wrapped in foil stamped with 'Not for sale, for the manager only'. We ate it on the loading lift of the refrigerated lorry, smearing it on baguettes and adding pig head sausage to it, washing it down with some good Bordeaux from a right-bank satellite appellation. We drank a little more wine than usual that afternoon. Kiwi Johnny, my partner in crime that vintage, said it was one of the best lunches ever. I couldn't disagree. The cheese was perfect; sweet, creamy, musty and decadent. It would have been the centrepiece of a cheese-board in any number of Michelin star restaurants, and yet there we were, stained, caked in grape guts, smearing great chunks of the stuff on baguettes whilst waving the flies away. Time stops for a lunch like that, and even though we know we have to get back to it, for a minute or two we could be anywhere and nowhere else. It's not about making wine, but working hard and rewarding that with something more than just a sandwich and a can of coke.

It's tempting to stuff your face, but as soon as you've refilled, you get back to the inevitable. Leftovers are squeezed into the fridge between half-empty bottles of wine and various bits and pieces. Glasses are rinsed with the hose and put somewhere they hopefully won't get broken. But they will get broken. The glasses in the winery always get broken.

Getting back into it after lunch is harder than starting in the morning. It takes a good hour to work off the food drowsiness. I try to make myself useful doing things that do not involve heavy machinery or precision. Sadly, there's nothing at the winery that doesn't require one of those things or both. That's also one of the reasons why it's important to avoid hangovers. Vintage involves constantly drinking and tasting, and the evenings involve beer and medicinal gin. Usually the exhaustion is too great for any large scale partying to be done. But then there are some nights that get away from you.

The hangovers stick to us like gum to a shoe. The night before involved fish pie cooked by Kirsten, too much wine, too many beers and quite a lot of whisky. Andy, Kiwi Johnny and I drank as though we had didn't have to work in the morning. It all started in the Sola with beers for Johnny and I. It was just a quick one. Then we popped into the wine shop to pick up a bottle or two for dinner before heading up to Andy and Kirsten's flat for dinner. Kirsten loves fish pie and crafts about as brilliant an example of the dish as you're likely to find anywhere. It tasted brilliant. We drank a bottle of Olivier Pithon's lovely white along with it, followed by one of Gauby's less expensive offerings, and before long felt the need to walk off the huge amount of food consumed. We went back to the Sola and then to the Templiers, where I might have fallen into an argument with crazy Ronnie. Gin and whisky happened. Andy managed to find us a cab back to Argelès. The drive back over the hills felt like an amusement park ride. Johnny told me later that I had an incredible discussion with the cab driver in spite of him not understanding a word I said.

Kiwi Johnny came to Scotland to play rugby. Along the way he wound up getting a job at Luvians, the wine merchant that was home to both Andy and myself for a while. Quite a while, if truth be told. In spite of coming from a wine producing country, Johnny's expertise was more based around beer and rugby. But he took to wine well, and when it came time to move back to New Zealand, he got a job at a local winery and started working crush (new world term for vintage) as well. Johnny has the itchiest feet I know. Any cash he makes gets put in a pot for the next trip somewhere. Africa, Asia, North America, Europe – I think next up is South America. He might even be there already.

He doesn't often retrace his steps, but making wine in France gave him a good opportunity to revisit some old friends in the UK while earning some cash to support the whole endeavour. So he joined us one year and busted his ass making good wine with us. That vintage we shared a flat in Argelès and ate a lot of pizza. The flat was tiny, with just a curtain to separate the kitchen from the sitting room and no bedroom door. We slept in bunk beds and were usually asleep by around 9-ish. Johnny was delighted to drink the big, rustic reds we made, as it made a nice break from the New Zealand Pinot Noir he was constantly exposed to. It was the year of cricket in the winery and Kirsten's incredible fish pie.

We sit at Coume del Mas and wait for the truck to arrive. It's bringing Syrah. I've drunk two litres of water and am still thirsty. Blinking hurts and the sun insists on shining as brightly as possible. It's not just the direct sunlight, but the reflection of it from off the sea and stones. I wear my sunglasses and speak little. My mouth feels like I've been chewing paste. Johnny shakes his head as it hangs low. Somewhere in the distance, deep in the winery, I hear Andy rummaging about. Sat in the sun on an old pallet, hoping for the rays to burn out the hangover somehow. It's just the three of us; everyone else is picking. Not us. We couldn't deal with sharp things today. No one talks, which is good. Occasionally one of us will sigh and comment about how dreadful we feel. I bury my face in my hands and rub the ever-accumulating sleep from my eyes. Andy has finished his rummaging and appeared from the cold room with three full sample glasses, all with a thin sheen of condensation courtesy of the cool liquid held inside. He hands one to Johnny and one to me and then swirls and sniffs the last one for himself. We do the same. It's rich and slightly sweet to smell, with clotted cream, pineapples and candied melons. It smells amazing. I take a sip and draw a bit of air over it, making that slurping noise that wine nerds make. The sip changes the world. It scrapes the glue from my mouth whilst invigorating my senses.

I don't know if it's a classic hair-of-the-dog situation, but within minutes, we're all feeling better. Andy took the wine from some reserve barrels put aside for an experimental bottling. It was all white from the Catala vineyard that we'd picked the year before, that afternoon I nearly collapsed from a more natural state of dehydration. It tastes like pure sunshine. After five minutes and half a glass, we start to resemble functional human beings again. We talk about the wine and how good it tastes straight from the barrel. It's 100% Grenache Gris, the strange grey/pink grape that gives this whole region some spectacular wines. Bolstered by summery nectar, Andy grabs a couple of barrel staves and a couple of silicon *bouchons*. *Bouchons* are the bungs we use to close up the barrels. Some are wood, some are glass and some are silicon. They frequently get lost and it's important to keep a stash of extras, just like the rubber washers for the hose valves. The extras are particularly important if you play winery cricket.

Winery cricket, as far as I know, is a natural evolution of shop cricket. Shop cricket was invented at Luvians in St Andrews, the small but extraordinary wine merchant that myself, Andy and Kiwi Johnny all worked at one point or another. Shop cricket consisted of fashioning a cricket ball out of several layers of the tissue paper we used to wrap up bottles, often formed with the aid of some packing tape and, if we were feeling industrious and focusing on detail, two thick strings would be stuck on as well, to act as seams. We had a yellow plastic toy cricket bat, and yellow plastic stumps. We set the pitch up to do the least amount of damage to the bottles of wine on the shelves. You might think it was a recipe for disaster, playing a stick and ball game in a shop full of expensive wine, and you'd be right. It was ridiculous, and there were many moments after a hard-hit six that we held our breath as the makeshift ball rattled off into the Burgundy shelves. But somehow we avoided disaster.

Winery cricket continues this long tradition of playing cricket where we shouldn't. Instead of a toy cricket set and a ball of tissue, however, it's a barrel stave and a silicon *bouchon*. We use the silicon *bouchons* because they bounce brilliantly. With no sign of our Syrah and a need to shake the boozy rust off, we double check the tanks to make sure the hats are all on, and set up with the batter standing in front of the cool room facing out towards the main door. We figure this reduces the chance of knocking the *bouchon* up into the attic where it will get lost among barrels of Grand Cru and Rancio Banyuls.

The *bouchon* is not round like a ball, nor does it bounce like a ball. It takes our dull senses some time to track the odd bounce and manage to hit it with any degree of accuracy. My job is to field on those rare occasions that Andy gets a hit.

Johnny's bowling. The few remaining empty tanks clang and echo loudly as the bung bounces about. Eventually I make a catch and Andy's out. I move to bowl, Johnny grabs the stave-bat and Andy fields. Johnny smacks one that bounces off the tank that's holding the Schistes, but we don't see where it goes after that. The day's getting warmer and we wander out into the sun, cricket on pause due to the missing *bouchon*. Along the road in the distance we see the Petit Forestier refrigerated lorry, full of our Syrah, winding its way towards us. We drain the glasses of wine and get ready to go back to work.

Most days there will only be one more lot of grapes in after lunch. The heat in the Roussillon makes it foolish, and a little dangerous, to pick too late in the day. Once those grapes are pressed or de-stemmed (white or red), then comes the every-thing else. If there are reds in tank, fermenting away, then it will be time for *remontage*. I like *remontage*. That's when you attach a hose to the higher valve at the bottom of a tank (called the racking valve) to a pump, and then take another hose and bring it to the top of the tank. It's called a pump-over in English. It's like stirring a stew, and you do it for a lot of the same reasons. When wine ferments, the yeast is respir-ing, creating a huge amount of CO_2. That gas pushes all the solids – the skins and few stems that avoided the de-stemmer – up, separating it all from the fermenting liquid below. That solid mass is called the cap. Being separated from the liquid causes the cap to dry out, and so what we do twice a day, once in the morning and once in the afternoon, is pump the wine over the cap to get it wet. This serves many purposes. Dried caps begin to smell awful. While CO_2 is protecting the wine, the cap is more exposed to the elements, so it could start its own little bacterial ferment and begin ruining the wine. It can also cause the wine to get too reductive, asphyxiating the liquid, leading to volatile sulphides and a nasty, eggy aroma. Running the wine through the cap alleviates this, and extracts more colour and secondary flavours from the skins. It also helps to aerate the wine, softening it somewhat and bringing out more elegant aromatics. Most importantly, it can be fun – there's something incredibly joyful about holding your hand over the end of the hose, pressurising the warm, fermenting juice so that you can reach all of the cap in the tank evenly. It's hands on; a tactile connection, quite literally feeling the juice as it turns to wine. And you can smell the change as you pump over; it gets fresher, sweeter, more perfumed as the juice wets the cap and they exchange between themselves. It can be a heady experience, and not just because of the CO_2 rising from the ferment (though that does mean you have to take great care at the top of the tank). Some wineries do five pump-overs a day. We do two. Our style is what's called 're-ductive' which means a lot of things wine, but for these purposes it can be read as anaerobic. We carefully control the amount of air the wine is exposed to, in order to preserve the freshness of the wine as well as reducing its exposure to potential contaminants. Reductive winemaking is something of a relative thing. We're very reductive in style for the region, the Roussillon, that we're in. If we were making modern Chablis or Alsace Riesling, we might be considered careless with the air exposure we allow.

All of our reds tend to kick off on their own. We don't need to inoculate with any particular yeast strain; wild ferments just sort of start. It doesn't seem to take very much time, either. I remember one 20 hecto tank of Carignan at Mas Cristine that exploded into ferment the very first night after picking. The tank fairly full, we gassed it with CO_2 (to prevent oxidation), put the hat on and inflated the rubber seal (think the inside of a bike tyre – now give it a metre and a half diameter, and there you go – it runs around the rim of the tank's hat, forming an airtight seal when inflated). We cleaned up, called it a day and most likely headed to Café Sola for a few beers and a bit of a chin wag with Laurent. Donald may well have been there, and he may well have shouted us a drink or two. If Donald was there, he likely introduced us to some new friend or acquaintance and perhaps we stayed a beer longer than we really should have. The next morning, we walked into Mas Cristine and it was as though a grape bomb had gone off. The hat from the tank was flipped over a few feet away from the tank and arising a good ten inches above the lid was the cap. All the skins and stems had risen to the top, pushed up violently by the CO_2 expelled from the respiring yeast.

In this case, the cap had risen a bit higher than it had room to do so. As well as blowing the hat off the tank, strewn around the winery sat clumps of skins and stems and small pools and streams of deep purple rivers, bubbling in places, finding their ways towards the drains. The winery was a bit of a mess. We set about cleaning up and came up with a genius plan to rack some of the fermenting juice into another tank so that the cap could settle without wreaking havoc upon the winery.

So that's what happens when reds start their ferment. They separate into two entities, the cap and the juice. As well as remontage to deal with the cap, there is also pigeage.

Pigeage usually starts before fermentation, and is the act of punching the cap down into the juice, and like pumping-over, it extracts more flavour and texture from the skins. As this can start before the cap actually forms, this is one of those jobs that starts off really easy: it's just plunging a long pole with a round, flat end that's covered in long prongs through a cool mix of juice and grapes, again, sort of like stirring a stew. Except it's plunging, not stirring. Then ferment kicks off and the cap rises. Sometimes it's easy. Sometimes you just put a bit of weight on the end of the pole, and there's a satisfying give as the prongs and pole disappear under the mass of grapes. The walls often give way at the sides, like when you dig a hole in the wet sand at the beach. There's not quite the childish glee that comes with spraying the hose in *remontage*, but perhaps a more physical satisfaction that comes from punching down the grapes. If you can. Sometimes the cap is too thick, so thick that you can stand on it and jump up and down on your *pigeage* stick and it won't budge an inch. That's when you get the hoses and pump ready for *remontage*.

One of the other jobs while waiting for fruit is taking the temperature and density readings of all the wines fermenting. This should be done every day. It's a long, tedious job. I remember hearing about one *stagaire* in Burgundy for whom it was their only job; barrel after barrel, sample after sample, morning until evening. It works like this: you take a 250ml graduated cylinder, a wine thief and the most fragile, breakable thing in the winery, the hydrometer, which is basically a weighted thermometer. You draw a sample from a barrel with the wine thief and pour it into the graduated cylinder. Because the wine is fermenting, it's fizzy, cloudy and foamy, steadfastly refusing to settle down. If it's Muscat, then it's also covered in Muscat scum, because that's what happens when you make Muscat; you get covered in scum. You then dunk the hydrometer into the foaming tube and try to read what the temperature is and what the specific gravity is. Usually there's a period where the foam obscures an accurate reading while the hydrometer bobs up and down like a buoy. It requires patience and a steady hand. I've not the latter, so I need more

[41]

of the former. The higher the specific gravity, the more time the ferment needs. The higher the temperature, the faster you run to either Andy or Philippe and ask them what the fuck you should do.

Specific gravity readings are particularly important for wines that are going to be fortified. At Mas Cristine, this will be the Muscat de Rivesaltes and Rivesaltes Ambré that we make, and at Coume del Mas it will be the Banyuls both red and white. Fortifying a wine is the process of adding very strong alcohol (in our case it's about 95% and comes from the distillery that we ship all of our *marc* to at the end of the day) quite early on in the fermentation to stop it in its tracks, leaving considerable residual sugar. In France, somewhat confusingly, this style is called *Vin Doux Naturel*. For all these wines, we tend to let nature do the initial ferment, due to fear that induced fermentation would be so strong that the spirit added would fail to halt it, leading to a bone dry, ridiculously strong and probably unpleasant concoction. With the Muscat in particular, the timing can be so sensitive that Philippe or Andy might, if the right point isn't reached at a reasonable hour, have to check up on the tanks in the middle of the night. One year, Andy had to pop in and fortify the Muscat at Mas Cristine at 4 in the morning.

The spirit for fortifying comes in large blue plastic barrels with two sealed holes on the top. The seals are official-looking, because they're officially sealed. As well as being a precise operation in terms of winemaking, fortification has to be reported in advance to the authorities. You can only buy fortifying spirit through official channels, and only in the precise quantities necessary for the amount of wine you intend to fortify. It's strictly regulated. Officials can show up on the day you declare you're going to fortify to confirm you're actually doing it. It's never happened on my watch, but the powers that be reserve the right to do so.

It's unnecessary with us, of course, because we're all lovely law-abiding citizens. But raw spirit is a potent thing, and in less law-abiding hands can be used to create any sort of hideous moonshine or counterfeit drink that took your fancy. Other regions that fortify often use a slightly softer, brandy-like spirit (Niepoort in Portugal get theirs from an actual Cognac house, or so I'm told). Regardless of where you are, the spirit must be as neutral as possible, meaning that all the depth and complexity comes from the wine itself, rather than what's added to it. In Portugal they refer to the fortifying spirit as the 'invisible hand', as its influence should be as subtle as possible.

The actual act of fortifying is just a manner of getting the pump set up with a hose going into the fermenting tank, and a hose with a long, narrow nozzle attachment like you'd find on the end of a hoover to fit into the blue plastic barrel. Pump the spirit through, let it all settle, and then take the measurements to make sure that the fermentation has been stopped and the alcohol levels are what they should be. If it's Muscat or Banyuls Blanc, it's quite simple, because they're white grapes and have been pressed straight off their skins after picking.

For Banyuls Rouge, it's a bit more difficult. You need to get as much extraction from the skins both before and during their very brief fermentation as possible. There's no luxury of several weeks bubbling away under a cap that gets daily showers in juice to get all the nuance and depth from the skins and pips. You've got to get your feet wet. When the must pump, which is the daddy pump in the winery, complete with the daddy hose, looking like a cyborg anaconda, finishes pumping the super-ripe Grenache Noir grapes into the tank that either the Galateo or Quintessence Banyuls will ferment in, a lucky couple of winemakers will rinse their legs with water and a bit of sulphur dioxide and get thigh deep into the tank to squish the grapes under foot. Feet are very good for squishing grapes. They tear the skins and release the flesh without tending to damage the pips at all, thus preventing the release of harsher, greener tannins into the wine. They do it this way in Portugal as well, though at this stage the grapes are put in shallow vessels called *lagars*, which are better suited for foot-pressing, and don't require ladders on the inside of a tank to get people out.

Up until the 70s, most of the wine from this part of the world was fortified, like Port, Sherry or Madeira. It is not a coincidence that these also happen to be very hot places to grow grapes. Fortification originated in these parts. As far as history knows, it was a physician named Arnaud de Ville-neuve, credited as a Catalan though born in Valencia, who came up with the process. Using Arab texts recovered from the re-conquest of Spain, he is the first known rectifier of spirit, successfully distilling pure alcohol. He worked out that by adding certain quantities of this potent, pure spirit to fermenting wine he could stop the fermentation in its tracks, preserving the sweetness of the wine but also retaining freshness and adding resilience to spoilage. All fortified wines subsequently followed this principle, be it Port, Madeira, Sherry or Marsala.

Villeneuve lived in an interesting time. It was the aftermath of the brutal Albigensian clearances and accusations of heresy on matters of both theology and scholarship were hurled in every direction. Being a heretic was much like being a witch in 17th-century Salem, or a communist during

[44]

the time of McCarthy. It was the preferred means of under-mining a rival's reputation. Villeneuve's scholarship made him controversial and a target. Often the accusations of heresy levelled against him would come while he was in service of the church in one way or another. It was, allegedly, the accusations of heresy from the ecclesiasts at the University of Paris that forced him to flee France for Sicily.

And yet in the midst of such controversy and various sentences levelled on his life by reigning clergymen and nobility, Villeneuve managed to achieve remarkable scholarship and practical application of his theories. His book *Liber de Vinis* was considered to be the definitive tome on the subject of wine; so much so that when the printing press was invented, it was the first book on wine to be printed on a wide scale and translated from the Latin to German. He lends his name to the medical school at the University of Montpellier and to several hospitals in Spain. And, appropriately, to a cave co-operative in the Roussillon (I've not tried their wines).

Villeneuve was, first and foremost, a physician. His work with wine, while extensive, was based on a fervent belief in its inherent medicinal properties. This was nothing new. Since the beginnings of winemaking, medics have spoken of its healing properties, millennia before having the ability to explain why it had healing properties. His belief in medicine and science often brought him into conflict with the church, and he was frequently in and out of excommunications, with popes and kings often trading pardons, shelter and notices. That he was held in high regard, even after his death, is indisputable. That it was his work on wine which was the first to be translated and printed using the printing press, in 1478, is testimony to that.

Of course, this being 700 and some change years ago,

there's some doubt as to whether Arnaud is the actual author of the text. Certain mediaevalists like to debate it. As a recovering mediaevalist myself, I can understand the urge to question sources and take certain attributions with a pinch of salt. It's a driving foundation of the discipline. I nearly fell into it as a career. That first wine job I took was meant to be part-time while I pursued a postgraduate degree in Mediaeval History. I'm often tempted back to that path, and wonder what would have happened if I had not strayed from academia to wine. However, this is not a mediaeval history paper. It's a story about winemaking, and for the sake of a story about winemaking, I'm going to assume that Arnaud (or Arnau, or Arnaldus) de Villeneuve (or de Vilanova, Ville-Neuve or Villanovanus) both authored the *Liber de Vinis* and came up with the processes and techniques that he's credited with. They say history is written by the winners; Villeneuve died in a shipwreck on his way to meet the pope. Make of that what you will.

Fortified wines are not as popular as they once were. In France, Banyuls and Rivesaltes used to be the most popular sweet wines in the country. This entire region's success and purpose was based on fortified wines. Dry table wines were an afterthought until very recently, and demand for them hasn't filled the vacuum left by the lack of market for the sweet stuff. The big co-ops don't really know how to respond to it yet. Whether they work it out or not remains to be seen.

Even as a small producer of high-quality wines, finding a market for fortified wine is difficult. It seems, at the moment at least, to be the territory for enthusiastic wine nerds, gaining little traction among the average consumer. The idea of sweet wine brings connotations of bad 70s Liebfraumilch or your granny's cream sherry. Simply getting people to give Banyuls a taste can be quite a task, and then there are the different classifications. There's 'Rimage' Banyuls, which would be called 'Vintage' Banyuls if the folks in Porto hadn't trade-marked the word 'Vintage' with regards to fortified wine exclusively to Port (you can't make this stuff up). *Rimage* is an old Catalan word for vintage. Grand Cru Banyuls must spend three years in barrel before it can be referred to as 'Grand Cru'. This is a more oxidative style of wine, whose closest comparison is probably Tawny Port. There's a lot of very old Grand Cru Banyuls kicking about, but be warned. Most of the years they put on the bottle are rough guesses at best, and often bear very little connection to the actual year of harvest. Frequently, the barrels will have been topped up with wine from other years. It's not through any malice or intent to deceive that these questionable years are put on the bottles, it's just that the wines were made in decades before having a specific harvest year was all that important to anyone, wine-maker and punter alike.

Last, but most peculiar, is Rancio Banyuls. This is the driest style of Banyuls, and comes from 'cooking' the wine either by storing it somewhere quite hot, or ageing it in glass *bon-bons* (a *bon-bon* is a large, rounded bottle, capable of holding sev-eral litres – it gets its name from its round shape, like a round sweet) and keeping it on the roof of the cave, allowing direct sunlight to cook the liquid. The result sits somewhere be-tween Sherry and Madeira, but is still remarkably 'Banyuls-y'.

All of the styles are unique, and within each one is a remarkable variety between producers and individual cuvées. Here's hoping the punter's palate returns to appreciating such wines before they disappear, or are reduced to simple curiosities.

BATTLESHIPS &
THE MIGHTY CLIO

IF COUME DEL MAS FITS THE IMAGE OF A SMALL
but perfectly-formed winery looking out over the Mediterranean, Mas Cristine doesn't... really... fit... at all. The
house that is Mas Cristine, with its beautiful rows of vines
surrounding it, gives us its grapes and name. Where we make
the wine is about three or four kilometres away from that
beautiful house, with its beautiful vines. Since we took over
the vines, we've been making the wine in a corner of the cave
co-operative in Argelès. It's an enormous building, probably
about two and a half football pitches in its entirety. And it's
falling to bits. Too many bird nests in the rafters. Built into
the structure itself are rows and rows of vast concrete vats
for making far more wine than they need to these days, the
majority of which have fallen into such disrepair that you
wouldn't consider putting liquid for human consumption
into them. My rough arithmetic makes me think that when
this place was fully functional you would have as much as five
million litres of wine bubbling away in these vats. Nowadays I
reckon that the co-op, who only have about four or five of
these vessels still functional, make about a tenth of that. Most

of their wine ferments in epoxy resin tanks, and quite often there's an odd odour that emanates from their side of the building.

The co-op looks like an old polaroid. Dust and cobwebs cling to everything, as does the black mould that feeds on alcohol vapour; it adorns the walls and looks like the scorch marks from fire damage. Anything left untouched for more than an hour or two will attract some manner of filth. If it weren't for the people working, and the odd smell of a bad ferment, you'd think the place was abandoned.

And there we are, in our small corner, squeezing in where we can, making (casting all modesty aside) fantastic wine in spite of it all. I like to think of the Mas Cristine team as the small mammals on a dinosaur carcass in the cold months after the big asteroid hit the Yucatan Peninsula. I love working in Coume del Mas; it's beautiful, and it seems sometimes that the wines just effortlessly reflect that beauty. At Mas Cristine absolutely nothing is easy. We don't fit in our space, so there's a refrigerated storage container for fermenting the whites. Most of the winemaking, the grape processing, takes place outside, because when all the equipment is inside, there's no room to work. There's barely room to squeeze from one end to the other. Working in the container, managing the whites and keeping them cold, is also an act of patience, pace and often better suited to a contortionist than a winemaker. We earn the wine made at Mas Cristine. It is all the more extraordinary that it exists than anything else we do; simply that we can keep the winery clean enough to prevent contaminants and the like is a minor miracle.

Please don't misunderstand me. Making wine at Coume del Mas is very hard, and the wine is rightfully brilliant. But Mas Cristine is like making wine on an obstacle course. And so Andy, Julien and I wear the work we do there as a badge of honour. And we sink a few more beers before clean up as well.

The first year I worked at Mas Cristine, we didn't have a big, shiny, stainless steel bag press. Nor did we have the traditional basket press, formerly the mainstay of pressing grapes in this region and now often reduced to ornamental status; found usually as decoration in the front of wineries throughout Collioure, Banyuls and the Roussillon. Instead we had a mechanical beast, a horizontal screw press (which is exactly as it sounds – it uses massive screws to slowly smoosh grapes together) painted yellow with burnt red highlights, but pockmarked and blemished with abrasions and patches of rust. The cylinder for the grapes did not have the precision-perforated side for allowing the juice to drip through evenly, but instead used a series of segmented wooden grates. It looked like something salvaged from a shipwreck, or that you'd find on *Scrapheap Challenge*. I called it the battleship, though I'm not sure why. It was yellow, not grey. Utterly dilapidated, it fitted in with the rest of Mas Cristine perfectly.

However, long after the battleship was replaced with our shiny new bag-press, it stayed there, resting and rusting just outside the doors to the winery. That also fitted perfectly. While other, prettier, less dangerous wineries had an old basket press in the courtyard, often turned into a large flower pot, we, in our crammed back corner of the cave co-op, had a rusting metal hulk decaying slowly among the tall weeds. We didn't throw it away for some time.

You don't throw much old equipment away. Winemakers are natural hoarders. There's always the fear that you might need it if something goes wrong. Some new-fangled piece of machinery might bite the dust right in the middle of a press cycle or just while you're cooling down a ferment, and it's beyond anyone's ability to fix it. At Mas Cristine, we stopped using the dangerous old milk tank for five or so years, but we didn't get rid of it. We stored it on top of the chill container, just in case. And then, one year, when the chill container broke, we got the forklift, brought it down, cleaned it up, plugged it in with crossed fingers, and were amazed that even though we'd left it out in the elements for half a decade, it still worked a charm. And it saved our bacon.

Even at Coume del Mas, there's the old equipment grave-yard. Around the side and in the back of the cave sit old tanks, odd lengths of hose, battered but functional pallets, cooling vats and an array of bits and pieces whose use is known only to Philippe. Every year I come back and half expect it to be cleared out, for there to have been a bit of a tidy in the winter months and all of that crumbling old kit to have been shipped out for scrap. But it isn't. It's still there, usually with a few more pieces added to the pile.

When something does go wrong, you try to fix it before phoning an engineer. Winemakers by necessity must be a combination of plumber, electrician and joiner in order to get through vintage. Time is too precious to waste waiting for a professional to get to you, and so very quickly you learn to grab a screwdriver, take whatever's broken apart, and have a look to see what might be wrong. Most of the time, it's pretty obvious. You see what's broken and you fix it, if you can. If it's beyond repair, you phone the engineer/professional and while you wait for them to show up, you fall back on your makeshift redundancy plan that you've figured out in the meantime, because you can't just stop because something's broken down. The 'how do I keep moving?' plan formulates alongside the 'what if I can't fix it?' plan. You rummage through the old equipment, or notice as Andy or Philippe grab some bit of kit that's sat unused for so long that you no longer recognised it as anything other than scenery.

I always thought that some day, in the midst of an epic technical failure, we'd be forced to clean up and make ready the old battleship for one last pressing whilst waiting on an obscure spare part to arrive from Italy, home of the shiny new bag-press. It had become as much a part of the scenery as the refrigerated container or the co-op itself.

And so the day that flatbed lorry arrived, complete with crane, was a bit of a shock. It was at the beginning of harvest that they came, and I looked in confusion and no small amount of wonder as the two blokes had a chat with Andy and Julien, and then began strapping up the battleship.

'I thought we were keeping that in case of emergencies.'

'What? Are you kidding?'

'No, really. What happens if the press breaks?'

'Rich, even if the press broke, we wouldn't have used that bloody thing. It was rusted on the inside, and the wooden grates were rotting.'

'Right. So why was it sat there for four years? I thought it was there in case of emergencies.'

'No, mate, it was there because we couldn't find anyone to take it away.'

'Ah.'

The crane lifted the rusting mass high over us and then swung it very slowly to the flatbed. I was sad to see the battleship go. It was a reminder of my start here, and of just what a challenge winemaking in this borrowed corner of the world can be.

The grass where it sat had died; yet another blemish on the landscape behind the large building in Argelès. To this day, when I look at that spot, it seems as though something's missing.

Sometimes Kirsten brings the boys to the winery. Andy will let Theo sit in the forklift and pretend to drive it. His legs are too short to reach the pedals, but he grips the steering wheel and pretends to honk the horn with glee. Sometimes he doesn't just pretend to honk the horn. Both he and Angus have big smiles, which makes it quick to forgive them when they get into mischief, which they do with regularity. They are wee boys, after all. Andy will hunt around for a tank that's still juice (that hasn't started its ferment) and draw two glasses worth for the boys. Theo, the older one, will make sure his dad's looking and try to swirl the juice in his glass and make a show of sticking his nose in it and smelling before he takes a sip. Angus, younger, still getting to grips with cups that aren't sippy, holds the glass by the bowl with both of his hands with Kirsten keeping a watchful eye and a hand close to the base of the glass in case Gus loses his grip. Baby Gus (Angus is not a baby anymore, and quite soon he won't even be toddler, but I have a feeling the name 'Baby Gus' might last a bit longer than its accuracy does – it's just too much fun to say) takes big sips, and excess juice dribbles down either side of his mouth. Theo holds the glass by the stem, and can wield it somewhat clumsily. Kirsten somehow manages to keep an eye on both of them as they sup down the grape nectar and then hold their glasses outstretched for more.

She tells Andy about one afternoon at home, while he and I were at the winery, Theo got very business-like, or as business-like as a three-and-a-half-year old can get. He grabbed his beach bucket and walked around the kitchen, picking up every corkscrew he could find and putting it into the bucket. Kirsten watched until he strolled over to the kitchen door and made to climb down the stairs. 'Theo, what are you doing?' she asked. 'I'm going to go to work with Daddy and Big Rich,' he replied.

We'll have a beer or a glass of wine during these visits. They're a welcome pause in the day, though when they finish it's like recess coming to an end at school. It's harder to settle in and slip back into routine when it's over.

Mas Cristine isn't just a strange place to make wine, but Argelès is kind of a strange town to be in to make wine.

Argelès boasts the best beaches along this stretch of coast. The stretches of sand in Banyuls and Collioure are more small pebbles than sand, and can be brutal on bare feet if they're not used to it. And just on the other side of the autoroute from Argelès, you have the foothills and forests; some truly stunning scenery. You're never very far from somewhere beautiful; romantic, even. As far as spots boasting scenes of spectacular natural beauty goes, the back entrance of the cave co-op, where we make Mas Cristine, ranks quite low in this part of the world. The building itself is a bit of a shambles: the dirt drive is pockmarked with craters and potholes, what greenery there is is the sort of scraggly underbrush you'd expect from somewhere more abandoned than this. Opposite the entrance and drive is a storm drain that curls underneath the raised train tracks that run parallel to the winery. Next to those tracks is a large, corrugated metal shed that holds various bits of disused winery equipment. And, of course, there's the large, ancient and battered refrigerated storage container that we cool the whites in during harvest.

And yet the drive outside our entrance sees its fair share of traffic. More than it deserves. Folks walk their dogs. There's an old drunk who hides his stash of terrible wine on a shelf, outside of the back of the container, where the controls for the refrigerator are. He rides his bike for his morning visits to the stash. He wears thick, grandpa-style glasses and pale blue shorts, and later in the afternoon he'll be pushing his bike along, leaning it up against the wall of the winery, too tipsy to ride it. He has wispy white and grey hair and a salt and pepper moustache that curls slightly, but isn't waxed, at the ends. Greetings are usually just a wave or a brief bonjour. There's a house next to the winery that has a fig tree. A few of its branches reach over their high wall and often the old drunk will pluck the low-hanging figs for an afternoon snack, having finished his tipple. If there are no figs, sometimes he'll show his disapproval at this lack of figs by pissing against the wall. Then he'll push his bike away home up the road.

The old drunk used to have a dreadful tumour on his nose. The effect made it look elephantine, and magnified the cracked red broken veins brought on by the cheap wine kept in a plastic water bottle by the container. Kiwi Johnny remarked on its anatomical resemblance, and thus dubbed the old drunk 'ball sack nose'.

A few years ago, however, the old drunk had an operation to remove the growth and fix his nose, and so, whilst the nickname lasts amid the giggles of winemakers and pickers who see him stagger past, it's no longer relevant.

Sometimes he'll stop and taste a grape or two. Sometimes we'll give him a taste of wine. He gets more surly with each visit and has been known, in the late afternoon, to push his bike past us with stagger, swearing at us under his breath. It's the sort of muttering anger of a paranoid drunk thinking that the world is laughing at him. To be fair, we've had a chuckle or two at his stagger home, though I doubt he's aware of it. There's a sadness to it all, which gives the chuckles a hollow echo. But if you couldn't laugh about it, you'd soon be looking for a place to hide your own bottle, somewhere a bike ride away.

The folks who live in the house don't like us very much. We turn the dirt track outside their drive into a potholed swamp six days a week for eight or so weeks a year. Nowadays we give them a case or two of wine to placate them, but still there's rarely a smile or a wave when they're coming or going. I always hold my breath a bit when I see them arrive home from work, slowly bouncing through puddles and potholes, gritting my teeth and hoping they don't scrape their undercarriage against the road. Feeling that at any moment, they'll lose it and unleash a barrage of Gallic and Catalan vitriol and bile in my direction. Still, they did decide to build their house next to both a train line and a massive winery. I'm not sure what else they were expecting.

While over the course of harvest the faces of those who walk and drive by the winery become familiar, there's another group of visitors that go unseen, but not unnoticed. Andy and I only know they exist because of what they leave behind. It turns out that our ugly little corner of Argelès is quite a popular location for the odd romantic liaison. For years we've found the remains of such encounters in the form of condom wrappers and, unfortunately, the used contents of said wrapper. These discoveries tend to result in a conversation that goes something like this:

Me: 'Dude, the most romantic person in the world took his date to an industrial wasteland again.'

Andy: 'He really knows how to show her a good time, I wonder if they had a drive-through at McDonald's before they had sex against a storage container.'

Me: 'I wonder if they even got out of the car.'

Andy: 'Taking a leaf out of your book, eh Rich?'

Me: 'I taught him everything I know.'

By this point I would have thought of a better response to Andy's ribbing, too late for it to be a proper retort. Instead I'll just shake my head and laugh. Andy will probably do the same. And then we'll wander away in disbelief, not wanting to dwell too much on our discovery and yet still mystified as to what manner of circumstance would bring someone here, of all places, for a shag.

One morning during a recent harvest I was driving into Mas Cristine for the day's work. Elysia was with me, a skilled and experienced winemaker from Western Australia with a superb nose and palate for detecting faults during ferment but a somewhat spotty memory for remembering which tank needed to be racked into which other tank (with often hilarious, though problematic, results, one of which lead to the creation of a new, one-off, and not terribly legal rosé). As I pulled the Mighty Clio into the drive outside Mas Cristine I noticed an old VW Polo parked beside the corrugated shed. The light was on in the car and as I parked, turned off my engine, and exchanged a 'what the fuck?' with Elysia, its engine creaked into life and it was off like a shot.

I felt slightly awkward that I'd interrupted something, but at the same time annoyed that that something was taking place at my winery. Elysia wasn't quite sure what was going on. I was fairly sure, and hoped that I was wrong. But it was only later in the day, when the sun was up and the press was running, that I found myself in the general area where the Polo was parked. And there I saw on the ground both a shiny, and empty, Durex wrapper and, about a car's width away a discarded, quite obviously used, condom.

More head shaking. They're all quite odd in the Roussillon.

One year, a bunch of us stayed in a house up in the hills behind Banyuls, just before you get to the wilderness. It was a nice place, with a patio, one of those brilliant barbecue chimneys that you find in gardens in the Med, and a big, tiled outdoor table. In the evenings, over a beer or a glass of wine, we'd sit at the table and play cards by the outside light. Sometimes we'd invite Olivier and Adele over, a couple who had worked both at Coume del Mas and Mas Cristine, and fire up the grill, cooking loads of spicy merguez sausages and the strange pork cuts that the French insist on calling bacon. They all smoked, as the French seem to do. Our chat was in pidgin French and pidgin English. Adele was adamant that I learn some French, and she was right to do so. She was patient though, they all were. Sometimes the conversation got quite serious and philosophical. They asked me about Obama and crime and Scotland and the wines that I'd tried. We spoke about all things, really. I was the oldest, and in many ways the most experienced, and yet I felt like a novice, held back a few years due to poor language skills.

Justin usually won those card games. An oenology student about to enter his final year at Toulouse, Philippe brought him in to pretty much run the winemaking at Coume del Mas so that he, Philippe, could spend more time in the vines with the pickers. Justin arrived for harvest with both his girlfriend and his brother. His brother only stayed with us for a short while, but on the odd day would help out a bit in the winery. Justin spoke better English than I did French, having worked vintage in California the year before. He made serious Cabernet for someone out in Napa and, as such, returned to France with a disdain for the both the coffee and the bacon in his homeland.

For most of the harvest, it was the two *stagaires* and me in that house on the edge of the wilderness. We looked over a valley to the hills that I'm fairly sure were in Spain. In the mornings before the sun rose, you could wander across the narrow road in front of the house and stare out there thinking that you were the only person in the world. It was a steep, zig-zagged, downhill walk into town for a beer. Along the way, you passed both a museum dedicated to the ancient wines of Banyuls, and the massive head office of the Cellier des Templiers Caves Co-Operative, the largest co-op in the appellation.

Mornings fell into routine quickly at the cottage. I woke first, just after five, to get to the toilet before the others. There wasn't much chat. Just the barest of *'bonjours'* between us, with perhaps the occasional *'ça va?'*, but the latter was unnecessary. We were all the same: tired and sore and not wanting to speak. We brewed a pot of coffee (terrible, terrible coffee) and put together breakfast. A bowl of cereal each and toast and preserves and sometimes fruit as well. We each had a glass of juice and a glass of water. French breakfast cereal became one of my cultural stumbling blocks. All of it seemed to have chocolate in it. The selection of cereals without chocolate would, in total, take up only about three or four rows on the shelves in the local Carrefour, if such a selection were set aside in its own right. It wasn't, and so I would spend hopeless moments looking like the most indecisive breakfast shopper in the world, looking for a box of healthy muesli that didn't undermine its goodness by having a large Toblerone's worth of chocolate in it. Soon it became apparent that it wasn't worth it, and my strategy changed. I went from seeking the cereal without chocolate to seeking the cereal with the most fucking chocolate imaginable. But not just some junk food crap; cereal that otherwise would have been considered healthy, but for its cocoa-based payload. That's what made me shake my head. It was like serving whipped cream with quinoa, or wrapping broccoli in strawberry Twizzlers. Eventually I settled on Carrefour's pure grain Alpine Muesli (no added sugar) with triple chocolate chunks. In fairness, it wasn't Cocoa Pops, it was proper dark chocolate. I remember seeing Kirsten later in the harvest for a catch up, and asked what cereal she bought.

'It's so hard to buy it in France; it's all just full of fucking chocolate.'

So she gets friends to bring her Crunchy Nut Cornflakes whenever they visit. It's not much healthier, if at all, but at least it's a little more breakfast-like.

We ate in silence, chewing and slurping and blowing on our coffee to cool it down enough to make it drinkable. The food was communal, but there was one of us who kept aside his own little brioche buns. After the rest of us had finished, he would remove one of the buns from its individual wrapping, butter it, and add some manner of jam. He bit into it slowly, and ate as we cleared the table. It seemed a little like an act of defiance. A relic of routine from a time before harvest that he insisted on maintaining, regardless of time constraints and the demands of the day ahead. Or the need to clear the table.

Sleep is precious. That year in the Banyuls cottage, it didn't come easily. My bed was a mattress on the floor in the sitting room. It lay perpendicular to the bed that was being used by the only *stagaire* I've met in my time there that never really seemed to get it. The brioche bun-eater. At night, when it was time for bed, he would phone his girlfriend and whisper to her for what seemed like hours. His tone was different on the phone, and he sounded too much like a bad, and somewhat whiney, Serge Gainsbourg tribute act on those calls for me to be touched by the romance of it all. Instead I would lie there, staring at the ceiling, waiting for the conversation to end before I could fall asleep. As the weeks of harvest drew on, I became more and more incensed by the routine, and my roommate's inability to do the courteous thing and maybe have the chat in the kitchen with the door shut, so that I could fall asleep. But I let it slide, at first because I thought maybe I was being a little judgemental. Later, it was because he'd proved himself to be such a galactic level asshole that I feared if I lost my temper about anything with him I might wind up killing him. It turned out that I was not the only one.

He studied in Bordeaux, and was from there. He spoke down about the Roussillon and its wines, and had a stereotypical *Bordelais* arrogance that seemed better suited for a comic book or a 50s English farce rather than an actual human person. Pretty much everyone I've met in the years I've worked in France has made me very fond of the French. They've been welcoming, generous, kind, helpful and very patient with my total inability to learn their language, even though I still dream in it (I had a French nanny in my youth, and was, according to my parents, pretty much bilingual until the age of about three and a half – since then trying to re-learn it to any useful degree has been fruitless, and I have tried). Having worked in the wine trade for well over a decade, I love the French. I love their wine, their food, their country. I even like their surliness. So coming face-to-face with someone who seemed to go out of their way to show off all of the worst of their reputation was a shock at first. I kept quiet about it to start with, but I thought the guy was a total dickhead.

I puzzled about this. We'd never had a total dickhead on the team. We'd had drunks on the team; drunks that needed to be sent home before they hurt themselves and others; people far gone in their life to a tragic level who needed help that we couldn't provide. So we put them on a train or a plane and sent them on their way. Vintage had to take priority.

We'd had English gap year kids who thought they would pick grapes for a couple of hours in the morning and then go lay on the beach and drink loads of wine for the rest of the day. They were lazy, but pretty honest about it. We put them on a train too.

But how do you deal with someone who just isn't a very nice person? Who abandons their colleagues in the middle of important work to go wander the winery, because they've become bored. Who seemingly takes everything you learned that you must do to make harvest work and just says, 'fuck that, I'm not doing it'.

I didn't have to work with him much. The first time we were paired up was on the bottling line. I folded boxes, he put the bottles in the box. It took us both awhile to get the pace right. Once we did, he just buggered off. He muttered something and I assumed he was just going to the toilet or something like that. It was only about 30 minutes later, as I poured with sweat and had managed to both fold and fill, that I realised he hadn't intended on coming back. This was early on, and I thought he may have been given another job and forgotten to come back to finish this one, or whoever was meant to help me out after he left was waylaid by some other disaster. I gave many benefits of the doubt. It was only later in harvest that Andy told me that he'd found him just wandering one of the alleys in the winery, nosing about as though there wasn't any work to be done. Andy, of course, gave him a bollocking and a different job, with him and José coming to help me out on the line.

As the vintage progressed, it turned out it wasn't just me that noticed the tendency to be work-shy and unpleasant in our colleague. Justin told me he'd do as little as possible, apart from drive the forklift at Coume del Mas like a rally car. At one point, he knocked a stack of comportes filled with grapes down the side of the hill. Having spent the morning letting Justin do all the work himself, he then begged for some help cleaning up the mess he made. Justin told him to fuck off and do it himself.

One day he went out with the pickers to do the porteur's job whilst they harvested the Macabeu for Mas Cristine Blanc. It's a big vineyard, the Macabeu vineyard, and it's brutal to pick. He did a dreadful job and offered no apology. When encouraged to pick up the pace a bit, he threw a tantrum, and started screaming and swearing that it didn't matter, it was all pointless, as all the wine in the Roussillon was shit anyway.

He finished early that year, and drove back to Bordeaux before anyone else finished. We weren't sorry to see him go. The cottage felt a little bigger once he left. The mornings were still quiet, but perhaps with a couple more smiles and an extra cup of coffee. Julien, José and Vincent will still, with a shake of their heads and a roll of their eyes, chuckle about his tantrum in the Macabeu vines.

It was my fault. The Mighty Clio, the rancid and filthy vineyard car that becomes mine during vintage, needed its French equivalent of an MOT, and I left the keys to the caravan (that vintage I lived in a caravan on a campsite in Argelès) in the driver's door pocket.

I don't know how the Mighty Clio passes that test every year. One of the doors doesn't work, the power steering's gone, the suspension seems filled with old sponge rather than hydraulics, and the brakes only respond once the driver's grim look of terror reaches the apex of contortion and his (my) knuckles are totally bloodless, braced for impact on the steering wheel.

Not content with being unfit for the road, the Mighty Clio smells. It reeks of sulphur products and guano so thoroughly that driving with the windows open in a 50-mile-per-hour wind (also around the Mighty Clio's top speed) cannot fully dissipate the stench. On those days where it's left in the sun and some numpty (me) forgets to leave the windows open at least a crack, climbing into the car is much like entering a poisoned sauna.

It's because of these things that it's the perfect vineyard car, and I'm really quite fond of it, from its bare, hubcap-less wheels to the mystery that surrounds whether you've put it into first gear or third, there's something brilliant about a car that you have to manhandle in order to drive. And you can throw it around as much as you want. You have to – some of the roads up in the vines count very much as 'off'-roading, and would shatter the wheelbase of many a better car.

Not so the Mighty Clio.

So this stalwart vehicle of the vines was sent, complete with our housekeys, to the mechanic, for what may well have been its final inspection before the car gods finally recalled it to the great scrapheap in the sky. I realised my mistake too late, and so my fellow *stagaire*, Elysia, and I were homeless for an evening. It wasn't all bad.

Andy and Kirsten kindly let us stay the night. We ordered pizza and sat up late drinking a nice Meursault. It was a premier Cru Genevrières from a chap named Francois Mikulsky. I'd bought it in Toulouse. Andy and Kirsten's flat has an art gallery on the ground floor; an *atelier* that Kirsten manages and hangs her art as well as that of a few other artists. That's where we sat while we drank and chatted and listened to music. We spoke about everything over the course of an hour or more, and often spoke about the wine. It changed through the night. Sometimes we talked about the art around us, sometimes the music, sometimes the liquid in the glass, usually after a lingering sip that showed something that hadn't been tasted before; a new flavour or feel. The wine opened up as the evening went on, as did the discussion. Andy selected a new playlist from iTunes and Elysia spoke of the huge wineries she'd worked in Australia; of 60,000 litre tanks exploding and the weirdness of night shifts during harvest (the heat in Australia makes night-harvesting a regular practice, and night-harvesting means night-winemaking). Kirsten spoke about her paintings and the herding of cats that is managing a gallery of artists and their egos. About the browsers who seem keen, and promise to come back with their chequebooks, never to be seen again. Folks who feel they're being polite, but are really just getting an artist's hopes up and letting them down just to save face; to make themselves feel better. It would be so much easier if they just browsed, smiled, said thank you, and left. Kirsten has a lot of cats to herd, between her artists, her two boys and Andy.

My turn came, but I didn't talk about baseball, because the Sox were having a wretched season. I don't know what I talked about; Andy either. I reckon Andy probably mentioned music, and I stuck to wine. I was thinking about other things, but probably stuck to wine.

We sipped all the way through, and as we crept towards the ends of our glasses we got quieter. It was late; later than any of us tend to stay up at vintage. Half the gallery sat in darkness.

[66]

There's always a whiff of oil paint in the gallery. It's good. It reminds you that something's made there. I swirled my glass again. I only had a sip left. I shoved my nose in the glass and raised my eyes at the others and smiled. They finished their glasses and I took my last sip as we all headed towards the stairs. I held it my mouth for a moment, tasting everything I could. The last sip is always the best.

TOMATOES & HALF DAYS

THE WHITES COMES IN FIRST — THEY'RE
pressed straight away and, if we're lucky, they're happily fermenting while the reds come in. The reds come
in and go straight into their tanks, and if we're lucky, they kick
off their ferments with little hassle. Throughout it all we're
cleaning, tasting, testing, fortifying, cleaning again, moving
equipment and making sure nothing's going terribly wrong.
That's harvest. Cleaning, lifting and making sure nothing's
going wrong.

And then there are Sundays.

Sundays tend to be half days. Pickers don't pick, but winemakers still have to mind the juice. There may be some cooling down to do, and no doubt there will be *remontage* on the
reds. Sometimes I have the winery to myself on a Sunday. I
work slowly, deliberately, on these lonely Sundays. Bungee
cords act in place of another person to help out, securing
both hoses and ladders whilst I switch on or off the pumps
and chillers. We don't have temperature-controlled tanks,
and so we use a great big cooling box that attaches to the
pump called a group that cools the wine down as it runs
through it. Lowering the temperature of a 5,000 litre tank by
ten degrees can take a few hours and ties up a pump for that
time. One year, the group broke at Mas Cristine. And then

[69]

the refrigerated container packed it in as well. This was while we were harvesting the whites, where temperature control is at its most essential. We were racking the fermenting white and rosé into old refrigerated milk vats to cool them down. We used a great deal of CO_2 to protect the wine from oxygenation during the constant racking and re-racking. A few of the whites at Mas Cristine kicked off their ferments wild-style as well (most likely due to the warmer temperature), which normally would be a nice thing, but that particular year just meant far more racking and cooling than two pumps and two milk tanks are able to cope with.

Coume del Mas is a bit nicer to work in by yourself. At Mas Cristine, the co-op workers don't come in on a Sunday, so it feels as though you're working in an abandoned factory. One that might be haunted. At Coume del Mas, it's not quite so unsettling. It's a pretty place and suits the quiet. The echoes aren't quite as ominous.

You take the temperature and density readings, hoping that nothing's hot. If something's hot, it slows everything down, and your half day might as well be a day as you wait on the group to cool down the wine. You taste on your own, that bubbling juice, and maybe give it a bit more thought than when you're in the rush of the week, knowing how much there is to do. Maybe you'll turn on the radio, and hope that it isn't too appalling (French radio is the pits). One Sunday, I'd just given up on the *pigeage* on the Mourvèdre tank. I hadn't been able to budge it; it was impenetrable. So I got the pump set up and made sure that I had a couple of strong bungie cords. The Mourvèdre tank stands next to the big, new oak fermenter, which has a convenient ledge that you can sit on while pumping over. It's a rare change from clinging to the top of a ladder. I was double-checking the pump sockets when the Petit Forestier refrigerated van arrived. Out of it popped Philippe and his eldest daughter, Fanny. We exchanged bonjours – Fanny was in her mid-teens then, and still had that lingering shyness around those older than her. A friend of Philippe's had some Muscat vines to pick, and Philippe volunteered his day off to help out. I mentioned the intransigence of the Mourvèdre and he backed my decision to do *remontage* rather than break my back attempting to punch it down. He said he was bringing the Muscat back here to press it with Fanny later in the afternoon, and told me where to leave the key when I left. He looked entirely content with the day as it was, picking and making wine with his daughter on an overcast Sunday. I watched as he grabbed a few things from the winery and jumped back into the cab of the truck with Fanny.

I finished pumping over the Mourvèdre and moved over to the small tank that held a mix of Syrah and Grenache in the corner of the winery just behind the south door. Small tanks make it hard to secure the hose when you have to work the pump, and there was a bit of kick back. As I turned on the pump, the hose leapt out from the top of the tank and managed to knock out a huge mound of grapes, and their juice, all over the floor and under Tank 1 (which holds the juice that will become Schistes). I continued the *remontage*, after a considerable barrage of swearing to cut through the peaceful calm of the winery. When I was done, I climbed down the ladder set about tidying my mess. I was annoyed at myself, in part because I'd not secured the hose well enough, but also because of the extra time added to my part day's work. I cleaned the mess, crawling under Tank 1 to get the clumps that had lodged themselves as inconveniently as possible. I put the ladder and the pump away, coiled the hoses and electrical cables and triple checked all the tanks to make sure all was in order. It was, and so I shut the barn doors and then locked the little one. It had clouded over while I worked, and the sky was grey out to the dark sea. There was no Tramontane wind that day, just the occasional whisper of breeze. It was not yet lunch time. I had the rest of the day ahead, and as I stared out to the horizon, the only thing on my mind was a long nap.

Occasionally, there really is a day off. A day when you don't go into the winery at all, when you can sleep past 5.30 a.m. and feel no guilt.

The first harvest I worked was a big one, and there was only one *stagaire* to help out. It meant Andy and I got a day off only once in three weeks. We drove out to the beach at Argelès Plage with plans for a day of swimming, frisbee, beer and maybe a nice bite at one of the places that wasn't too touristy. Kirsten was pregnant with Theo, and had gone to Scotland during vintage, so it was just the two of us. We found a spot near the water and lay out the towels. I muttered something about having a quick nap first. Sunscreen liberally applied and Sox hat pulled low over my eyes, à la Indiana Jones, I lay back, closed my eyes and slowly the sounds of the crashing waves and the folks playing in them faded into silence.

I didn't dream. The volume rose again and I lifted my hat to find Andy towelling off from a swim.

'How long was I out for?'

'At least an hour. I fell asleep too. Needed to dive into the water to wake up a bit.'

'An hour? Am I burnt to a crisp?' I sat up and poked my legs and chest to see if there were any of the signs of burning, but couldn't really tell. The idea of working in the winery with severe sunburn filled me with dread.

'I don't think so.'

'Can't believe I slept that long. Best get in the water.' I ran down and dove straight in, hoping it would wake me up a bit. It's one thing being exhausted at work, it's entirely another to be exhausted on your day off.

The water gets quite deep quite quickly at Argelès. It's not like Collioure, where you can walk out 20 metres or so without slipping under.

I got out and Andy was packing up. I didn't blame him. The swim had given a jolt, but falling asleep in the midday sun doesn't make you especially keen to stay out in it. I was annoyed. I think we both were. Wasting a precious day off to nap. Nap in style, perhaps, on a beautiful white sand beach in the bright and burning Mediterranean sun, but nap nonetheless.

Since then I've taken more care about my days off during harvest.

They can be lonely mornings, because those that you're not working, someone else has to. If I'm in Collioure, I'll walk over to the Sola and sit in front in the morning sun, order an espresso and a petit déjeuner. It's nice to eat and sip and see the people in their morning routine – it makes a nice change from shuffling through the streets in the dark, munching on a pain au chocolat as you go, all while everyone else is sleeping. The Sola's a bit of a different place in the morning. It has free wifi, so it becomes a bit of a Babel, with multiple nationalities tapping away at their laptops or Skyping loved ones. And you'll always get the hardcore sports fans, sitting inside in the main bar, watching either the highlights from the day before or rugby live from the other side of the world, depending on the time.

I like petit déjeuner. It's simple. A nice strip of baguette with butter and jam, some yoghurt, hopefully with fruit compote, a croissant with more butter and jam, a glass of orange juice and perhaps some fizzy water. Moving in and out of the winery on most days, you can forget just how bright and clear the sun can be in this part of the world. Breakfast at the Sola serves as a good reminder. If I'm out for the day, I put some sunscreen on my arms, legs, face and the tops of my feet. You only have to burn the tops of your feet once to never forget to put sunscreen there ever again.

If it's a Wednesday or Sunday, the market will be on in the square next to the Sola. It's a good market, with a superb fromagerie and a brilliant tomato farmer. In the States they'd call them 'heirloom' tomatoes and in the UK they might be referred to as 'heritage'. All manner of colour and shape, they look like nothing you'd find in the supermarket and taste of such concentrated juiciness, that you don't really need to do anything to them other than eat them. If the tomato guy has enough, that's the salad for dinner sorted. Little bit of salt, olive oil and good vinegar and it's one of the tastiest things in the known universe.

So I wander around the market and nibble some samples from the pretty girl selling cheese. I stare for a while at the paella dishes, a metre and a half in diameter, filled with rice, seafood, spices and a cornucopia of vegetables. I'm always somewhat fearful of these dishes, wondering just how much they can sell in a day, and how much of the old gets blended into the new. Probably none, but I still can't shake the thought.

Cured meats of all shapes and forms, bread stalls with towers of loaves whose crusts are still crackling as they settle. Tables laden with local honeys next to ones with all pickle or preserves. In the far corner of the square is the 'stuff' section, where all manner of crafts and trinkets can be purchased.

I tend to give this area merely a glance. The sights, tastes and smells of the victuals are far too much too ignore for long. The market is one of those brilliant things that brings everyone one out: local, expat and tourist all mill around doing their shopping, nodding and saying bonjour. A couple of wineries sometimes ply their wares, but you're better off checking out the vinegars, olive oils and other bits and pieces.

It's great to have a day off at the market because it means as well as that you can really spend some time on your dinner. Dinner at vintage is frequently as simple as lunch at vintage: bread, cheese and meat with a bit of salad. There's not much time or energy to do anything else.

Laden with cheese, tomatoes, rare cured meats and whatever else has taken my fancy (later in the harvest you start getting some incredible mushrooms at the market), I'll drop the shopping off at Kirsten and Andy's place and head back out. Collioure's a lovely town to not have to go anywhere in particular in. Usually I'll trace the line of the harbour, first by heading out to the end of the pier.

To get to the pier you pass the main church with its iconic steeple and the small chapel on the beach. If I were in the UK or back in the States for this sort of walk, I would pop my headphones in and wander about to my own soundtrack. But I like the noise and the bustle here. I don't speak the language very well, but I love to hear it. I can't bear to block out the sounds of the sea, either. So I walk with my eyes and ears open, sometimes with my big camera, hoping to see something I haven't seen before.

The view of Collioure from the end of the pier gives a great sense of how dwarfed the town is by the hills that surround it. The church, the fort, the windmill and the mysterious castle that sits high above the town, owned apparently by a Parisian millionaire, are all in view, jutting out on their various ridges, hills and peninsulas. You can see down the coast as well, towards Cap Bear and Port-Vendres, though it's just cliffs and rock that meets the eye.

I take it in for a few minutes at the pier's end. Having lived in St Andrews for almost two decades, I've grown fond of stone piers, and cannot see one without the desire to travel out to the end of it, its furthest stretching point, and look out to what sits further.

There will be a steady stream of people doing much the same, though they don't tend to linger as long. They get to the end, tick the box of 'done that' and head back. Sometimes I'll look up to the hills and the vines at Le Rimbau, wondering if anyone's picking up there.

From the pier I'll head back into town at a slow pace. I'm not in a rush, and I know where I'm going. I walk along in front of the touristy tapas bars on the stony beach, serving the hungry and thirsty in their hundreds, dodging children loose on school holiday, marvelling at the French habit of taking tiny dogs for a walk by carrying them, instead of walking them. Depending on the day, I'll walk up by the Templiers and back towards the Sola to see who's about. If I'm hungry, I'll just cut across the bridge by the fort, and take the walk along the water, past the fishermen and painters and the stand that takes bookings for boat trips.

By this point it isn't just the sun that's hot, it's the light bouncing off the water, and the heat reflecting off the stones and sand. Everything is warm.

This path takes me to the other side of town, to the good beach and the carousel. I pass them all, and wander instead all the way around, towards the SCUBA school, and to the steps of Les Voiles.

Les Voiles is the bistro of the Neptune, once the Michelin Star flag-bearing restaurant for Collioure. It sits on a short cliffside about eight metres above the harbour. You sit outside, but are protected by 'sails', strips of cloth that serve to keep the most ferocious of the sun at bay. It's the only tourist-y place that I like going to in Collioure because it's got the best view, the kitchen is better than the others and because it's not on the main strip, it never seems as crowded as the others (even though it's always full). And the service is good, and friendly, even. Sadly though, in spite of much pleading on my part, there's no access to the Neptune's far superior wine list from here.

I get a table with a view out to the pier and order a pichet of rosé and some fizzy water. The menu is much like the others around here, but I don't mind. I get something fishy and then something meaty. Or something meaty and then something fishy. The cured boudin noir is particularly good here. They've got groovy wine glasses, and I like picking mine up by the stem and holding it out to the coastline, looking at the world turned upside down through a vinous filter. Looking at the cracked, cut, calloused and tannin-stained fingers of my vintage hands as they grip the perfectly formed vessel that holds a liquid, the making of which no doubt caused someone else's fingers to look exactly like mine do.

I'll take my notebook out and do some writing, taking my time with my lunch. Sometimes I'll pick up my camera and snap a shot of an interesting boat making its way into the harbour. Mostly I just try to be there. To listen, see and feel my surroundings, set in that perfect small spot. To taste as the wine scrapes the food from my palate, amplifying it and being amplified by it.

I don't usually get cheese or dessert. Just the bill and a

coffee. Then maybe a walk up to the moulin above the gardens that sit behind the museum, the one that I've never seen open.

Around six, I'll head over to the Sola again, to meet Andy and Kirsten and the boys. We'll have a beer and then turn the fruits of the market into some manner of a meal.

It's nice to be drinking a beer and to be clean, fresh and not in too much pain.

LADDERS & HOSES

THE LAST BIG WINEMAKING JOB OF VINTAGE
is pressing the reds. Once the ferment finishes, without
the cushion of CO_2, the cap falls back into the wine
and sinks. The fermented juice picks up added complexity
and depth, but you don't want to keep it there too long as
the stalks and skins can contribute too much, leading to over-
extraction and tannins that will never soften. For some reds,
we'll press before the ferment has finished. This leads to a
lighter, fresher and more fragrant styled wine.

But for the most part, in the quest to remain true to the
grapes that thrive on these terraced hillsides, we make big
wines, which means we press after ferment. This is often an
adventure.

First off, we strain the free juice off the cap. This will go
into either tank or barrel, depending on the grape and cuvée.
Usually our Syrah goes into barrel and our Grenache goes
into tank. This can be a fairly simple, if careful, process, and
quite often gravity does most of the hard work, with the pump
only coming into use when absolutely necessary. We need to
be careful with the pump, as if solids from the cap make it
through the strainer, it can muck up the works. As for the
strainer, well, it's basically a big sieve or tea strainer that holds
back the solids of the cap. Once all the free juice is racked
into its new home, that's when the fun begins.

If it's one of the smaller tanks, 2,000 litres or so, it will be on a pallet, which is good as that means we can get the forklift ready. Before we get the forklift, however, first we have to get a ladder, because someone has to get in the tank. Barefoot, with feet and legs rinsed in a mixture of water and sulphur dioxide, they climb a ladder, usually with a shovel and a length of cut off garden hose to use as a snorkel, just in case there's any lingering, suffocating, CO_2 hiding at the bottom of the tank.

Once in the tank, standing atop the mound of skins and pips and stems and lees (dead yeast cells) that takes up about a third of the volume, the wine-o-naut (frequently me), will give the thumbs up to the forklift operator and up the tank will rise so that it is above the door of the press. With the tank on the pallet on the forklift perfectly positioned above the door of the press, the wine-o-naut begins to push the muck out through the door at the bottom of the tank.

It's disorienting being the wine-o-naut. Usually the tank is stainless steel, and the acoustics manage to amplify every-thing, but also absolve it of all direction. Every noise comes from 360 degrees and though it's loud and echoing, it also seems from a distance. The humming pneumatics of the fork-lift and the sense of lifting outwith your own power. All you can see is a distorted, curved reflection of yourself atop a mound of grape guts; above you is just the blank ceiling of the winery. The team outside shout at you, making sure you're ok and not suffocating. You shout back that you're fine, louder than you really need to, because you think you're further away than just a few feet. You feel further away.

It's disarming to see the grapes beneath you suddenly begin to slip away, seemingly into nowhere. It's like standing atop the sands in an hourglass. The folks outside have opened the door at the base of the tank and so starts the outpouring into the press. Gravity only goes so far, and so you use the shovel to push the sticky mass towards the door. It seems somewhat antithetical to survival instinct, to work so hard to get rid of the ground beneath your feet, but even so, you stick to it. As you go you get more careful. As the weight at the bottom of the tank shifts out, the tank becomes more precarious, and your weight becomes far more influential. Leaning too much to one side or the other could result in a drop and quite a lot of damage. By the end you're on your hands and knees, grabbing the last handfuls of skins and sliding them out. Afterwards, the forklift lowers you down and someone hands you a ladder so that you can climb out. The sun's brighter, and people's voices sound a little clearer.

If it's a big tank, you still need someone in there, there's just no mucking around with forklifts. Nope, instead you fill the big red comportes with sticky cap and load them into the press by hand. Very similar, in fact, to how you made the whites about a month ago, but a lot more messy. And no fucking bastard comportes. They're hole-y, and would waste wine.

Pressing reds is heavy work. Once the press is loaded, the remaining juice is squeezed out from the cap. Press juice is aged separately from the free run, just as with the whites we age the higher pressure pressings separately. Bizarrely, our press juice often tends to be a lighter, more floral and elegant sort of wine than our free juice. In a region like Bordeaux for instance, the opposite is true, and in most wine producing regions it's the case that the juice from the press is much like the last bit of coffee in a cafètiere: backwards and wince-inducing.

Once the reds are all pressed, which can take a fair few

days, and the press is sparkling clean (cleaning the press after the reds sucks, and requires an awful lot of hydrogen peroxide), then it's time to breathe. The wines are in their élevage stage. Maturing and eventually undergoing their malolactic fermentation. There's a party, but unlike many wine-regions, there's no bubble-gummy Nouveau to swig. Instead it's beer and plentiful wine from the previous year. Julien Grill, one of the partners in Mas Cristine and owner of many vines, knows some guys who do incredible spit-roast lamb, rotisserie style, slowly rotated over hot coals for a good three or so hours and so succulently tender that it just melts in the mouth. José, in charge of keeping the vineyards in beautiful shape, will bring some of the world's finest cured meats from over the border in Spain and, if everyone's really lucky, Philippe will be on hand with the Roquefort in the special foil. The weight of the last eight weeks is finally lifted, and while there's still much to be done, the work now is with wine rather than grapes. But for perhaps a few parcels of late harvest vines, whose rich, sweet, sugary raisins will provide for weird and wonderful dessert wine, the harvest is done for the year.

With the winemaking done comes the cleaning. Cleaning after vintage is sort of like cleaning at the end of the day during harvest at the winery. Some days, during harvest, the pickers at Coume del Mas will work a split shift. The winery crew love it when they do. It means that the pickers head home for a siesta while we in the winery press or de-stem or whatever work the colour of the grapes dictates for that day. And then, as the last press cycle winds down, noisily exhaling the last of its compressed air, or the last comporte full of Grenache Noir is unloaded onto the escalator and dropped into the de-stemmer, the *vendangeurs* return from their naps and start taking apart the equipment and moving it outside

[82]

the cave to get it cleaned. These are good days, because they tend to mean that I get out of two or three hours' worth of cleaning and I get to drink beer sooner than normal. Mas Cristine does not have such luxury of staff, and when the winemaking is done for the day, the cleaning begins, and it's the winemakers that have to do it. However, usually by the time cleaning starts, Julien, who owns and manages most of the vines for Mas Cristine, has cracked open the beers. Julien loves the beers. He's a proper, rugby-playing Catalan who looked the proudest I have ever seen anyone when he left the winery early one day to watch his six-year-old son's first rugby match. His and his father's vines provide much of the fruit for Mas Cristine, and it was through him the whole resurrection of the label happened. It was Julien that first heard that the lease was becoming available for both the vines and the label itself. He approached Philippe as a winemaker and a third guy (who I never met, as he is *Champenois* and spent most of his time up north, making wine with bubbles) to form a partnership. It was after their first vintage together in 2006 that Philippe realised they needed a winemaker to run Mas Cristine with their full attention, as Philippe couldn't do both (the harvests overlap too much). All this coincided with Andy finishing his winemaking course in New Zealand and want-ing to make wine in France. So Andy joined the band that Julien had put together in the first place.

Julien's work is essential and his work ethic is admirable. But most importantly, Julien makes sure there's always beer at Mas Cristine. I remember one year, a few vintages under my belt, sitting on an upturned comporte at the end of the day and drinking a cold wee bottle of Heineken or red label Kronenberg, and telling Julien the Australian saying, that it takes a lot of beer to make good wine. He loved it. He brings it up every year now. And I love that before I start cleaning up, I can swig on a cold brew.

I can't begin to express how important cleanliness is in a winery. I've mentioned it before, I know. It's the least glamorous secret ingredient in the world. A filthy winery can do all sorts of terrible things to a wine, be it microbial infection or general contamination. Any winemaker will tell you their job is to express their *terroir* as honestly as possible – none of them want their wine to taste of something that went wrong in the winery. And so everything gets cleaned.

To be honest, cleaning goes on throughout the winemaking, it just intensifies once the day's winemaking finishes. Throughout the day, you're rinsing comportes and cleaning tanks and barrels. Big wineries have a proper barrel cleaning station, where you insert a pressurised water gun into the bunghole and spray it clean. After that you burn a sulphur candle in the barrel to clear out any microscopic bugs that the water cannon may have missed.

Comportes get sprayed at high pressure and then left to dry out in the sun. Cleaning big tanks requires 'product'. Product is essentially a heavy-duty alkali cleaner, and breaks down to two strengths. Really strong is caustic soda. Less strong is hydrogen peroxide. You have to be super careful. Gloves and goggles, or at least sunglasses. In the new world, after using caustic, they then rinse with citric acid to neutralise the alkali (caustic/citric is the phrase they use). In France, citric acid is strictly regulated in wineries to control use when acidifying wine. Therefore, you can't really use it as a cleaning product. So instead of using caustic, we use the hydrogen peroxide, we have to rinse it with loads and loads of water to wash it clean. In order to spray with 'product', you attach a special jug to the end of the hose, like the sort of thing you'd use if you were fertilising the lawn. These jugs were engineered by the lowest bidder, and as such have the annoying tendency to explode in the face of an unwary winemaker cleaning a tank. It can be very satisfying though, hugging a ladder leant against a two or three storey high fermentation vat, spraying around the sides in a circle and watching as it dislodges the clinging sheets of tartaric acid crystals. They dislodge in massive sheets, which is good, as it means you won't have to climb into the tank with a scrubbing brush and get it off yourself.

Tanks are easy. The press, the de-stemmer: the machinery that makes wine can be extraordinarily difficult to clean. When the final press cycle comes to a halt, after the shrieks of decompression, you clear away the tray and grab the shovels. There's about a ton and a half of stems and skins to fling into the back of the truck. This is called the *marc*. If you go to a wine producing area of France, the local brandy is usually called '*Marc de* (insert name of region here)'. Around these parts, it's *Marc de Banyuls*. That's because all these stems and skins are loaded into a truck and shipped over to the local distillery to be made into spirit. The distillery also weighs how much you bring and compares it to how much wine you produce. If there's a discrepancy, you get fined.

We get fined a lot. Frequently during harvest, the last press won't finish until well after the distillery's shut for the day, and having piles of stems and skins rotting outside the winery isn't terribly good practice, so we'll dump it in a field that we own and spread it as fertiliser later in the year.

Then you get ready to go in. It's always unplugged for cleaning. I take off my boots and socks; some folks strip down to their skivvies. Crawling underneath the stainless steel drum is always awkward. You rise up through the hatch into the drum itself. It smells of grapes and stems and there's very little light.

[85]

All you're armed with is a hose. There seems an endless amount of pips and skins squashed flat surrounding you. As much as possible has been emptied, but there's always remains. There are folds in the inflatable leather bag that hide large handfuls of detritus. At first you spray hoping to stay dry, but under pressure and encased in steel, the water droplets find you and soon you're soaked to the bone and now you know why some of them strip down to their underwear to do this. You blast the hose along the seams of metal and leather, through the grate, deep into the hole on one side of the drum that always holds far more than you think. You herd it all to the hatch and push the piles of it out onto the ground. Once every thing is clear, you lift yourself up fully into the drum, so that you're crouching in it, bent over double, and you slide the hatch door as closed as it will go without slicing the top of the hose off. As it slides, it scrapes against all the pips and skins caught in its tracks. Spray and slide, spray and slide, dislodge and clear out every thing that you can. You won't get it all, no one ever gets it all, but you have to get everything you can see, and you have to know where to look to see. You double check to make sure, knowing that the first thing the next morning, if you haven't cleaned it right, that's when the boss will know. He'll open the press for the first load in the morning and see a pile of crap that you were meant to clean out, and already your day is off to a shitty start.

If you've done reds, there's the de-stemmer, escalator and sorting table to clean. These are a pain in the ass. There are hatches and valves and gears that need to be double and triple checked. The crazy baton-staff core of the de-stemmer needs to be removed from the machine and seen to separately. It's time-consuming, meticulous work. But you don't have to crawl into anything. You don't have to close yourself into a stainless steel drum and keep the thoughts of the bag inflating accidentally, even though it's unplugged, at bay. It's just a massive fucking pain in the ass.

When everything's clean, then everything gets put away. At Coume del Mas it just all rolls into the winery and is set where it needs to be for the next day. At Mas Cristine, there's more precision needed, as the press barely fits in the winery. Putting it away properly can be delicate and frustrating, because all you want to do at that point is go to the pub. It's like a jigsaw puzzle, making sure that the press goes in exactly right, and because it weighs over a ton and only one set of wheels swivels, there's a lot of trial and error, especially at the beginning of harvest, rolling it back into the winery. By the end of harvest, it tends to come a bit easier. You have to be careful though. An inch or two off mark and one of the press legs has fallen into a drainage channel and you need a car jack to get it out again. But once it's away, and the refrigerated container is locked, and the large, weathered doors to the winery are sealed tight, you can go to the pub.

We groan as we lift ourselves out of the white Modus. The parking lot sits on a hill that overlooks the centre of Collioure, and splits the town in two. There's a fortress built on the side of the hill that faces the sea. Part of it is a museum and part of it provides training facilities for the French marines. They train frequently. Like most hills here, it's a schist outcrop whose bare stone is dusty, whose grassy bits overgrow quickly, but in a straggly way, and whose trees vary. One of the local families grazes donkeys on the grass. It gives the donkeys food and keeps the grass tame. Watching the shepherd herd them from wherever up to the hill is quite a sight, stopping traffic on the main road and attempting to communicate with his flock in fits of comedic, eccentric flails and shouts. I don't think they listen to him. They only respond to him physically pushing them. Somehow he gets them from the hills by the border of Port-Vendres through the southern part of town and to the patches of grass above the parking lot on the hill. He smiles and laughs along the way, dressed in battered but whole clothing, tanned, deep creases in his face from laughter and squinting against the power of the sun by the sea. There's something dusty and happy about him.

Andy grabs his laptop bag and I sling my rucksack over my shoulder. We're filthy. Grape skins and pulp and pips stick to our clothes and flesh. I barely lift my legs, more shuffling than walking, relieved that we're making our way downhill. I allow gravity and momentum to provide energy as I barely have any. The hairs on my legs are matted in great clumps, stuck with grape must. My arms hang heavily, and I open and close my swollen fingers and feel the rusty creak of their joints as I try to keep them loose. The weight of the comportes will twist them permanently if I'm not careful. Tourists wander up the hill, returning to their cars, and regard us with curious glances. We both look like we've jumped on a grape grenade. The must has hardened the leather of my boots so that they barely bend at the toe. The soreness is general and pervading. There might be a cut or a bruise that shrieks to its own tune, but more a cumulative ache. So much of winemaking is cumulative, it's fitting that so too is the pain that comes with it.

Andy measures vintage by how far into it he starts taking painkillers before he goes to bed and when he wakes up in the morning. At the foot of the hill, we stagger into the Café Sola and Andy heads to the bar to order the beers. His French is better than mine by a factor of about a million. He also gets a local discount. I smile at Laurent, the manager, who sits at

[88]

his regular table with an empty coffee cup in front of him. He likes asking how I am in English, and smiles broadly at my answer in broken French. The answer is always some flavour of 'bon'. I used to only order small beers, or *'un demi'* at bars in France, because I was proud that I knew the word. After a day in the winery, though, it's *'distingués'* for us, though if it's me ordering, Laurent asks if I want a pint.

I'm a beer snob. Always have been. I drink ale and craft beer and rare bottles from small breweries. I like beer with flavour and think the average lager you find on draught in the pub is a hideous abomination.

All that goes out the window in the Sola after a day in the winery. I slurp down Heineken like a drowning man gasping for air, as though it were the very nectar of the gods.

Andy and I chat about the day and the grapes and the wines and the tanks and the barrels and all that has gone on since we woke. Then we'll notice the sport on the telly or whatever dreadful music they're playing and laugh about what it reminds us of. Sometimes I drink my pint too quickly and get brain freeze from the chill of the beer.

I could stay there until I fall asleep, pouring cold lager down my throat until I lose consciousness. So much of me wants to do that. But Andy has a family, a family he barely sees over this time. He needs to see his boys before they go to sleep, to eat with his wife and share some moments together before exhaustion takes over. It occurs to me that as the years have gone on, and Philippe has spent more time in the vines during harvest, that it's because he finishes earlier, and can spend more time with his family. I see Andy when we get home from our beers, high-fiving and hugging his wee boys, asking Kirsten how her day was; calling her darling, and look forward to him being able to pull back a bit himself. Let me

[89]

or some apprentice run the winery at Mas Cristine while he can see his family more during harvest time.

After dinner Andy and I popped over to the Sola for a beer before bedtime. Collioure was quiet, and a cool breeze bit at my bare legs. I don't tend to wear long trousers down here, and sometimes I regret it. The Sola was almost empty, and I didn't recognise the teams playing rugby on the big screen. On one empty table stood a giraffe; a five-litre tube with a tap on the bottom, usually filled with draft lager. It looked like a very tall bong. About an inch of sad-looking lager sat at the bottom of it, fizz-less. There was no sign of the giraffe-drinkers; they'd probably sought livelier surroundings. They'd most likely be disappointed. We sat inside and an older guy, maybe in his early fifties, joined us. Andy knew him. He looked well-groomed and respectable with that permanent tan that comes in these parts. He spoke softly with Andy and I couldn't quite follow – I knew it was about harvest, but not the specifics. Seeing I was struggling, Andy started to translate for me. The man had vines, passed on through generations from his family. He was talking about how much things had changed at harvest. As recently as 50 years ago, he said, his parents were harvesting with donkeys to carry the grapes back. One vineyard was a problem, however. It sat on the cliff-edge on the end of one of the peninsulas. The only road to reach it wasn't a road at all. It was a single track, and precarious at that. They could go and pick their grapes, but they couldn't bring them back. Instead, they needed to use a path down to the water at the base of the vineyard and wait for a boat to come from the co-op and collect the grapes from them. If the Tramontane was in, and the white horses were galloping across the water, it could be tricky for the boat returning with the grapes. Andy relayed the story with respectful amazement, and I listened with wide eyes. I'd seen the old tools of viticulture; my mind wrapped around the basic difficulties of wine-making in the past with little problem or shock. There wasn't a huge gap between how they used to do things and how they do things now. But the image of manoeuvring baskets full of grapes down a cliff side to a waiting boat threw into sharp relief not only how things had changed, but the lengths, in any era, that folks went through to get the harvest in.

We bought the guy a beer and listened some more. He doesn't have as many vines these days. Every year it's more work for less money. He doesn't trust the co-op anymore. He's not sure there's much of a future for small growers in Collioure, Banyuls or anywhere in the Roussillon, really. Andy nodded and said something that sounded commiseratory (not a word but it should be). It was a story Andy had heard quite a bit, and even I knew the narrative somewhat. The wine world down here changed quickly, and there are lots of people unsure of what that change means, or even how it's changed. What some winemakers find exciting, some grape growers find terrifying. What's certain though, is that even though people don't need to carry grapes down cliff sides anymore, it hasn't really got any easier.

The night before, I threw my old boots in the bin across the street from Andy and Kirsten's flat. The vintages had destroyed them. I needed to buy a new pair before next year. There was going to be a next year. After all that, there was going to be a next year.

Kirsten drops me at the bus stop and it's still dark. I've got ten minutes to spare and the Red Sox are playing their last game of the season. This month that I've been making wine, they've tanked their season and it's all come down to this one game against the Orioles. I'm waiting for the Frogbus to take me to Girona, and from there I'll fly to Prestwick and make my way to St Andrews after a brutal six weeks. I've not seen a game since I got here, and everything I've read is bad news. My data streaming bill's outrageous already, but I check my phone anyway. We're up. Paps is closing. I lose signal. I don't know what's happened. The bus pulls up and and I load my kit on, show my ticket and find a seat. My phone flashes back into service. The Sox blew it. The season's gone. Over. And I'm flying home. This one nearly broke me. It nearly broke me but I wanted to stay longer. It's not over yet. There's still wine to make. But it is for me. The Sox are done and I'm done.

SHRIVELLED GRAPES & BASEBALL

BY THE BEGINNING OF NOVEMBER, THE FER-
ments are all finished and the wine will be settling
down. Sometimes there's a small vineyard with shriv-
elled, but not desiccated, grapes left on the vine. They're
practically raisins. One year, on November 11th, Andy and
Philippe had such a vineyard, planted with Syrah. They
picked it by themselves. The grapes had a potential alcohol of
about 18.5%. They were left undamaged by rot or any of the
other nasties that can hit grapes that have hung on the vines
too long. It was cold but clear, and the work delicate. Grapes
in this state must be treated with a gentle hand. It took them
most of the morning. The wine they were making wouldn't
be fortified. They would let it ferment out naturally. It took a
year to finish that ferment, and when it did, it was still sweet
to taste. The yeast couldn't handle all the sugar and so they
gorged themselves and died leaving plenty. It wasn't a table
wine by any means. It didn't fit any standard classification for
sweet or dessert wine in the region. Instead they used a more
generic catch-all. A *Vin de Pays*. Well, actually, *Vin de Pays*
isn't usually permitted to be sweet, so you have to classify it as
'*Vin de Pays de la Côte Vermeille Vin Naturellement Doux*'.
They named it Armistice, after the day they harvested the
grapes. There was barely enough of it to fill a barrel.

Those Syrah vines have never again yielded such great, late fruit, but every year now, sometime in November, Andy and Philippe will find some good, late fruit, and harvest it. They treat it gently, letting natural sweetness shine through. One year it was Grenache Noir, one year Carignan. They always call it Armistice after that first harvest. They're rich, sweet wines and are best when enjoyed in quiet contemplation. They mark the last of the year's harvest. And while Andy and Philippe never set out to intentionally make sure they're never the same twice, I like that that's how it worked out.

At this point, the ferments have finished, Armistice is harvested and the new wine is resting and (hopefully) beginning its malolactic fermentation. Malolactic fermentation occurs when lactic acid bacteria in a wine convert the malic acid into lactic acid, releasing CO_2 as a by-product. This can be, and is, induced at larger wineries, but most of our wines kick off their secondary fermentation on their own. The effect is to soften the wine somewhat, as malic acid is sharper on the palate than lactic acid. Not all wines undergo this secondary fermentation, in fact, quite a few wineries go out of their way to prevent it, as it can undo fresher, lighter styles – especially in whites. All this is a technical way of saying that even though the ferment is finished, the new wine is still doing stuff, but it's stuff that it needs to do on its own.

With the new wine doing its thing, and not needing pump-overs or punch-downs, and little of anything except a bit of lees stirring and tasting every once in awhile, this becomes a time of reflection. The serious reds from the year before now need attention, having rested in barrel for their duration, it is now time for them to be blended into the wine that will be bottled. Up until now, the separate varieties and parcels have been aged individually in barrel, as have the pressings. Up until now, much of what's been done is down to necessity. The techniques vary from winery to winery, and every plot of earth is different, but the path that's travelled is one that's dictated by scientific necessity. Geology, biochemistry, quite a bit of maths, that sort of thing.

Come November, Philippe blends the big reds, sometimes with Andy, and sometimes on his own. It depends. Those post-vintage weeks can leave a vacuum for a winemaker. There are some years when Philippe will get bored and drive over to the winery and build his Quadratur and Abysses on his own. Going from barrel to barrel; tank to tank with the wine thief and a sample tube, blending free juice and press juice, looking for balance and expression. I've mentioned it before, but I should say it again: Philippe knows what he wants from his wine. His wines speak directly of the ground they're grown in, and the fruit flavours are a means of transmitting that. I'm sure he deliberates internally about all this, and when he tastes with Andy and I, there's discussion and quite a lot of nodding and um-ing and ah-ing. We're lucky in that the wine is rarely bad or even middling. It's usually really good; but the goal is to make great wine, not really good wine. Sometimes the difficulty comes with a wine that is excellent but doesn't necessarily play well with others. Blending gets quite creative here, and the answers, when they come, are thankfully quite clear. And the answers I'm talking about are flavours. This is a nice point when winemaking really does have the odd Eureka moment.

My first experience with blending a cuvée, I didn't get to do it by committee. We were too busy. When there is no Eureka moment, when there's no getting a square peg into a round hole – or in this case, a couple of dozen barrels of Carignan to finish its ferment and settle down, sometimes the best option is to just leave it. Remember that ridiculous tank of Carignan that kicked off its ferment overnight, blew its lid off and covered much of the winery at Mas Cristine in chunks of inky purple fruit matter and pools of fermenting juice? That Carignan wasn't finished messing with us; not by a long shot.

As eager as it had been to burst into fermentation, it seemed less so to finish the act. By the end of harvest that year, analysis came back from the lab that there was still quite a bit of sugar left in it. We pressed it anyway, and racked it into barrels, hoping that in its new homes, the wine would finish its journey and ferment dry. Bottling a wine with too much sugar can be disastrous – a secondary ferment could give you an unpleasantly fizzy concoction. The only way to avoid such a thing is to basically nuke it with sulphur. And we didn't want to do that. So we left it for a year, sitting there in barrel, watching it undergo its malolactic fermentation, occasionally sending samples to the lab in the hopes that perhaps the sugar would suddenly disappear. It slept through the winter and even the warming temperatures of spring and summer couldn't wake any dormant yeast. We inoculated every once in awhile, using yeast strains the likes of which are used to ferment the ridiculously high alcohol wines from places such as the Veneto in North East Italy, and Napa, for its crazy Cabernets. All to no avail.

So one rarely quiet afternoon during the following vintage, whilst we awaited fruit or the end of a press cycle – or both – Andy took me aside and asked me to choose five barrels of the Carignan and make a blend. The rest were to be racked into a tank and, within legal limits, blended into a fermenting tank of the new vintage.

I was nervous. Don't get me wrong, I have confidence in

my ability to taste and assess both finished and pre-bottled wines with relative accuracy and usually a good sense of critical awareness. But that's judging wines that I'm being asked to buy and assessing whether me, or my customers, would like them. This was a different situation. I was being asked to make something, something out of a decidedly troublesome batch of grapes. And they weren't my grapes. It was Andy that asked me to do it, but it was Philippe that was going to have the final say.

Vintage doesn't do nervous, not really. If you know how to do something, you go do it. I know how to draw and taste samples from a wine thief, so away I went.

The wine thief at Mas Cristine is one of the big ugly plastic ones. There's no need for a 'nice company visiting' wine thief as we don't let nice company visit the dilapidated co-op (nice company taste Mas Cristine at Coume del Mas). That in hand, I grabbed a glass and gave it a rinse under the pressure hose, giving it a quick sniff afterwards to make sure there were no lingering smells. Want a surefire way to spot a wine geek? They sniff every glass before they put something in it. Trust me. I also picked up a piece of chalk for marking barrels good, bad or ugly. I didn't really know what I was looking for, so I went through them all once without making any decisions.

All the barrels were a year or more old. Various shades of purple stains surrounded the bung holes. They were only stacked two high. For some of the ones on the bottom row, it required a bit of contortion to draw samples. No two tasted the same. I sniffed and tasted and spat. It was sweet, viscous and woody. Their tannins rasped throughout my mouth. The worst managed to be too sweet but thin at the same time. The best seemed complete, or full of promise. Plums, black-berries, red apple skins immersed in spice, cinnamon, anise and gripping oak. There was something intensely purple about every taste.

That first walk through I marked eight barrels. The second walk through, it came down to six. I grabbed one of the larger sample tubes and made a blend of the four I was certain of; the ones undoubtedly superior. The resulting concoction was tasty but a little too in your face; a little too ripe and without anywhere to go. It lacked complexity, though it was very delicious. I wanted my blend to have complexity. I poured the tube into two glasses and topped up each with a small amount from the undecided barrels. One of the two barrels was more of the same – sweet and complete. The other was a touch more tannic, a touch sharper. A bit of that rasp, but without the meanness that had accompanied some of the others. It was the second I chose for the blend, looking for balance in an inherently unbalanced wine. I poured the first blend into one of the emptier barrels and put together another version of the second, hoping for a bit of confirmation. It tasted right. It tasted, to me, like a young wine. A wine that needed to be bottled and aged for a couple of years and then enjoyed with an incredibly hearty meal. The sweetness didn't choke you. Its length was good. It wasn't my kind of wine, one that I would seek out. It was a bit heavier than that. But I liked it. I poured a glass for Andy. He liked it.

I grabbed a sample bottle, one of the small ones we send to the lab for analysis, and wrote 'Carignan' on a sticky label and stuck it on the bottle. That was for Philippe to taste. I was to bring it to Coume del Mas for him to try on my way back to Banyuls. Instead, he showed up at Mas Cristine to pick up some other samples for the lab and took a moment to taste my little concoction. He poured a small glass and gave it a proper swirl and nose. I know a lot of folks find that pretentious;

two movements that instantly mark a wine snob in a crowd. Winemakers make it seem the most natural thing in the world. They swirl and sniff with intent and without any airs or graces. There's no nonchalant flick of the wrist for the swirl and they don't close their eyes for the sniff. Often their brow is furrowed. They don't talk while they're doing it, spouting notes on the colour or smells that they're getting. They swirl to coax as much out of the nose as they can, and they sniff to see what it gives them. They do it with furrowed brows, usually looking for what's wrong before enjoying what's right. Philippe holds his tasting sip for a long time, swishing it in his mouth to the point that he's chewing it. He draws air over it, sucking it through his teeth and then chews away at it again. Sometimes it looks, after he's drawn the air, as though he's puckering to kiss someone who isn't there. To me it seemed like he tasted it for a good few minutes. He spat and looked at Andy and said '*bon*' and then looked at me with a big grin. As seals of approval go, it was a good one.

So that was that. My wine was approved. It was going to be a thing. We racked those barrels into a small tank, added a couple of sulphur tablets and sealed it up. The unchosen barrels we racked into another tank, warmed it up, and added some yeast in hopes of finishing the ferment in a *pied de cuve*, or at least getting it started again to blend it in with the new vintage, which was already bubbling away. My weird sweet thing would be bottled as it was.

That year was a big harvest, and it took me some time to recover. It was in the aftermath of it that I came up with the idea of writing this book; of letting folks know what winemaking was really like. Not long after that, Andy emailed me a couple of photos. They were bottling that day, and what they were bottling was my bizarre Carignan. I didn't know what it was going to be – whether it was destined to be a Tramontane bottling or what. Instead it had been chosen for the Consolation range. That's the range we have for strange wines that don't really seem to fit anywhere else. They tend to be intense, small-batches that may only appear every two or three years, when conditions are just right. Armistice is bottled as a Consolation wine. This would be a new wine for the range, complete with a new name. He and Philippe had decided on 'Red Socks' as the name for the cuvée, and credited me with its creation on the back label. The photos he sent were of the front and back labels. I lost it a bit with pride. I emailed, tweeted, Facebooked, phoned everyone I knew that would give a shit about such a thing, and some who didn't. Most probably didn't, really. I would have told more, in more ways. I would have signalled folks by semaphore and Morse code if I knew either of those things.

I'm from Boston, and though I've lived away from there for almost a quarter of a century, I still follow the Red Sox with devotion that borders on maniacal. Mornings during vintage start with me checking the score of the night before's game. If they're playing on the west coast, the game may still be going on. I'll stream it if I can. In 2004, at around 5 a.m., I watched in a computer lab in the University of St Andrews as they won their first championship in 86 years, and subsequently phoned my father, who had served as a batboy for the team in the 1951 and 1952 seasons, and told him they'd finally won. All of my siblings phoned him that morning. If you were to meet me in person, in passing, I'd be wearing a Red Sox hat. I'd be able tell you the score the night before without issue. During the season I spend many an evening watching games into the wee hours of the morning, cursing the five-hour time difference between London and Boston. Harvest usually takes place during the most crucial month of the season, September. It takes my mind off the stress and frustration that the end of baseball season can bring, but also makes me feel somewhat disconnected from the team that I love.

By naming the wine 'Red Socks' (the other spelling is a registered trademark, and our little wineries don't want to get sued), Andy and Philippe tipped their hats in a far finer way than if they'd simply called it 'Richard's Wine' (or something similarly awful). I used to joke that if I ever owned my own winery, I would call the cuvée MFW (My Fuckin' Wine). Red Socks fits that bill perfectly. I never would have thought of it, and I can't thank Andy and Philippe enough for it. The first vintage of Red Socks was 2010. There was no 2011, but the 2012 is being bottled as I finish this book.

Once wines are blended, they are given time to marry, sometimes back in barrel, if they need it, and sometimes, usually, in tank. This extra time is important. The components need to interact if there's to be harmony in the finished product. From a practical standpoint, the longer they marry, the more complete the blend becomes through diffusion. From here, much in the winery is finished until bottling. From here, the winter draws in and the work moves out to the vines for pruning.

CATHARS & ELEPHANTS

I FIRST VISITED THE ROUSSILLON IN JANUARY. IT
was black, quiet and cold the morning I left Scotland for
Collioure. My breath hung in the air and the pavement
frost sparkled under the yellow streetlights. In the distance
waves crashed. Leaving Scotland in January for the south of
France seemed ideal. It's good to travel early in the morning.
It gives the sense that everything will be where you left it
when you get back.

The taxi driver's chat barely pierced my tired ears while an
old friend sang on the radio.

I made it down with little hassle. I visited Coume del Mas
for the first time and met Philippe. I made a note of the wines
tasted, and marvelled at how deftly he clambered over barrels
and the like.

Wines tasted at my first Coume del Mas visit:

Folio 07 barrel
Folio 07 tank sample
C'est Pas du Pipeau Roussanne/Vermentino 07
Syrah Mourvèdre Rosé (CdM Farniente) 07
Carignan Barrel 07
Syrah Barrel 07 [later to become Armistice]

Mourvèdre/Syrah/Carignan 07
Lunch at Philippe's – Quadratur 2001

Winter here is rarely cold. Having spent several winters in
both New England and Scotland, winter in the Roussillon is
mild, even spring-like in comparison. At least in terms of
temperature. It still looks like winter. Sometimes, it even
snows. Snow can be good for vines. It melts slowly, irrigating
the vineyard at a steady rate and doesn't run off as much as
rain can do on these dry hills. Sadly, snow doesn't hit these
parts very often, but when it does folks tend to be optimistic
about the coming harvest.

There's no snow this particular January, so we head inland,
into the hills.

An open restaurant at this time of year is a bit of a rarity,
but we find one and the gentleman is overjoyed to serve us.
Rillettes to start followed by an entrecote steak. Andy teaches
me how to order medium, which would be rare in any other
part of the known universe. I've since grown fond of the
rustic, slim steaks in this parts of France. Tough and toothsome but full of flavour as well. The frites are skinny and with
a pleasant crunch. We're the only ones there. A pichet of red
appears and we drink and chat about the place. I discover the
local version of crème brulee: crème catalan, which is crème
brulee with a hint of orange.

After dessert, there's coffee, and it's pretty bad. I grimace but
Andy assures me it's actually pretty good for this neck of the
woods. I'll never understand how the French can love their
coffee roasted so dark. It tastes as though it's been cremated
and mixed with the contents of an ashtray.

The vines we pass are between pruned and unpruned.
The tendrils of the unpruned lash whip-like in the Tramon-

tane wind. Vines are deciduous. Old vines in the depth of winter are bare, twisted, skeletal and fossil-like. All of their colour and vibrancy has gone, leaving them looking like de-saturated, lifeless husks. Their dried, crunchy leaves fly far in the harsh winds that rush down from the mountains. Driving inland up into the hills feels like driving into a black and white photo. The forests are still green, but not so you'd notice; you'd swear they were just a darker grey. The hills and mountains all stand jagged, looking like heaps of shattered stone piled precariously. It's quiet. I look out the car window and my eyes trace the line of one serrated peak that looks like the lower jawbone of a dinosaur. Some of its teeth jut out strangely, and for a moment I think I'm seeing things. A fortification; a tower almost indistinguishable from the points around it. I raise my camera to my eye and through the zoom I can even work out the masonry. It's not one tower, but several. Deserted. It's a castle. It belonged to the Cathars.

We park the car and get out. My eyes stay on the castle as we wander a vineyard of young Mourvèdre vines. They've been pruned recently, perhaps only the day before, and look now just like grey stumps reaching up from the fragmented topsoil. The sky feels low. Those peaks and towers look more and more to me like a skeletal jawbone, discarded in a colourless desert. The image is eerie, and I'm very aware of the lack of breeze. The vines around me could be arms of the undead, frozen shortly after they'd broken through the ground that served as their prison.

I remember the Cathars. Not personally, of course, but I studied them and The Albigensian Crusades that saw their end. There's something haunting about standing there in that valley, among the raw and naked vines, the only sound is that of shards of stone under foot. Staring up at the shell of a castle, knowing its inhabitants had been starved out or burned. Or both.

Eight hundred years ago and the emptying of this region under the banner of crusade was such that it never refilled. Many flocked to the Cathar cause, and were punished for what was viewed by the church as heresy. Even the Count of Toulouse, one of the most powerful nobles in all of France, bowed to authority in the end, renouncing his protection of the Albigensians. The remarkable mountain strongholds they built provided incredible, but temporary, protection. For 20 years at the beginning of the 13th century, the French crown, with the blessing of Pope Innocent III, flushed the Cathars out and, not entirely coincidentally, vastly strengthened its influence in the Languedoc and lead it closer to Catalonia. Villages nowadays are far apart and quiet. The folks here farm and grow vines, though each year it's harder. Many come from elsewhere, seeking solitude, and they find it.

In classical times, the Greeks traded along the coast. Then came the Romans and the Narbonne Province. It stretched from the coast up to Toulouse and the hills. Grapes were grown then, as was everything else. It was the Romans that built the terraces, steps on which to grow things in the hills without losing crops to the flash floods that came with the rains. It wasn't just vines, but olives and fruit and the like. Vines were important, though. As well as producing grapes for wine, they served as a sign of immortality. Stone coffins for the dead bore intricate carvings of grapes and vines and olive trees; symbols of life to take through to the next world, whatever branch of mythology that next world bore resemblance to. There's a museum in Toulouse, near the university. It's a treasure of a museum, small but perfectly formed. It used to be a mediaeval dormitory, and stands on the ruins of a mediaeval hospital. Next to it towers St Sernin, an awesome, in the proper sense of the word, cathedral whose architecture represents both the classical and Middle Ages.

The Musée de St Raymond (everyone in mediaeval Toulouse was named Raymond) is well-situated, considering the cellar itself is an exhibit. The floors above hold countless marbles and mosaics, dioramas and artefacts, but downstairs are tombs, casks and gravestones. The classical brick that constructed the ancient city surrounds you, and the remains of an ancient hospital wall bisects the lower level. It has the damp stench of the old that somehow manages to be both musty and somewhat cleansing. Most of this room is devoted to the dead; it's like an abandoned necropolis. The inhabitants have shuffled off this mortal coil, leaving only their final dwellings behind; their tombs and headstones, graves and those precious items seen fit to bury them with. An ancient wine glass sits on a glass shelf, dating back to the 5th century.

I found myself there by accident, wandering in a hush. I paused often to take notes and photos. The vine carvings on the ancient caskets held fantastic symmetry, though I sometimes mistook olive branches for grape vines. After a time I began to see the difference between them. Much like in life, the wine grapes tend to be round, while the olives were elongated and oval. Also, the leaves on the vines were much larger and broader than the olive leaves. Every tomb coats death in the ideal of so much life: wine and food and revelry. Wild boar hunts are depicted, reminding me of the gunshots that echo from the hills at harvest and the broad smile of our neighbour at Coume del Mas as he would show off the carcass of the huge beast. Not a bit of it would go to waste. They use the whole pig down here.

This unbroken connection to the past often goes unmentioned and un-noted amongst winemakers. Sure, they know wine has been made here for millennia, but it's not something that drives them. It's the season that drives them; that yearly cycle that leads to the reaping of the fruit and then its shaping into something else. It's for nerds like me, those with one foot in and one foot out of this remarkable business, to look into how those working the vines now are doing much the same as those who were doing it a 1,000 or 2,000 years ago. And it's likely that the cyclical, repetitive nature of it all is what accounts for both its longevity and its relative lack of retrospect. It's not just cyclical, it's continuous. Pausing too long to look back and admire the course of their history is a luxury that winemakers can seldom afford.

It's like pruning itself. The act of cutting back the vine harshly to promote new growth, the sort of growth that, weather, fates and wee beasties willing, will bring forth great fruit in the next vintage. There's little point in reflecting on those bare tendrils getting snipped and dropped. Either left in the vines as a very slow decaying fertiliser, quietly feeding future vintages, or they are burned in great piles at the end of the rows for the ash to be spread as fertiliser. Those bonfires smell quite sweet; they are as much a part of winter here as frost in the mornings and snow atop the peak of the Canigou.

Along with the Romans came the enemies of the Romans, and it is thought by some historians that Hannibal brought his armies and elephants along this craggy coastline to avoid the mountains and take advantage of the natural resources surrounding the area. I was told this story, not in winter, but during harvest, by Kris, the hippy Australian that helps in the vines and works his own grapes. He was basket-pressing his white grapes outside of Coume del Mas in the late after-

noon sun when he told me the story. A retired classicist/
archeologist had told him the story. Hannibal crossed through
the river valley that Banyuls-sur-Mer sits upon. This retired
scholar mentioned that the terraces dated back that far as
well, though many of them were used for fruit orchards and
olive groves rather than vine training. I never met the man
himself; I heard about him from hippy Kris. Hippy Kris knows
a lot of people because he's friendly, speaks a couple of
languages, and does that Australian thing of not being horren-
dously socially awkward. Hippy Kris is also one of the reasons
the Mighty Clio smells as awful as it does: one of his mystic
bird guano fertiliser tubs spilled in it (and probably some
other mixtures of his own creation). He chats, and expects
you to chat back, and when he engages in conversation, he
expects it to be that, not simply an exchange of greetings
designed to feign interest. He's interested.

So standing there, cleaning whatever it was I was cleaning,
while he spoke about this morsel of information, it seemed
utterly obvious to me that Hannibal had done this very thing.
I'm not going to check it. I have friends who are both arche-
ologists and classicists and could probably confirm in an
instant whether it's accepted as likely or not. They wouldn't
say whether it's true or not, but they'd say whether it was
probably true. The further back you get, the more that's how
history works.

But I don't want to check. Not because I'm enamoured of
believing hippy Kris or his retired professor, but because
I'm enamoured of that being one of the stories of this place,
whether it's true or not. It was a beautiful afternoon, and in
between tales of Hannibal, Kris debated quite seriously with
himself whether to add a sulphur tablet to his press juice.
It smelled funky and yet he really wanted to be as non-

interventionist as possible. We talked a bit about it, while I turned out towards the dry river bed that runs beneath Coume del Mas. The Med had turned its late afternoon topaz and the deepening sun saturated the green of the leaves on the hills that framed that small wedge of sea. Maybe it was a different river bed, not the one in Banyuls, but this one. Maybe over 2,000 years ago, young Rome's greatest threat lead his Carthaginian army, complete with its remarkable elephants, right by this very spot. His scouts may have used the very hill I stood on as a look-out point.

My mind wanders when I'm cleaning.

Hippy Kris told me the retired professor lived in the back woods behind Banyuls, where the wilderness starts. There are still vines there – some wonderful ones in fact, but it's a bit out of the way.

Kris smelled and tasted his press juice and broke a sulphur tablet in half, dropping it into the wine with a fizz. They work just like Alka-Seltzer. We kind of nodded and went back to our work. There wasn't much else to say. I cleaned and looked out to the valley again and thought of a column of elephants.

As far as I'm concerned, as far as Banyuls and its little corner of the Roussillon go for me, Hannibal passed through. He probably caused quite a ruckus, and no doubt availed himself of the local wines. They would have been a far cry from what we'd consider wine. Tradition at the time was to sweeten and infuse. Indeed, as there had been prior Greek influence in the region, they may even have added seawater to certain wines. It might seem strange, but I still love myself a glass of good Manzanilla, which is about as close to drinking seawater as you can get without actually doing it.

Carthaginians and Cathars in one region, separated by a millennium and change. It sits well with me.

The wineries lie quiet at this time of year. Often they'll be packed with pallets of empty bottles, waiting for the bottling truck to arrive. Philippe and Andy will pop in once a day to make sure the tanks are sealed tight and to taste. Sometimes there's blending to do, but that's usually sorted earlier on, in the middle of Autumn, a month or so after the harvest.

The equipment of vintage is packed tight and the floor of Coume del Mas becomes something like a jigsaw puzzle; the press, de-stemmer and elevator all carefully fitted away to take up as little space as possible. Climbing up to the 'attic', the space above the chill room where the grand cru wines are aged, you'd think the cave was more a storage garage than a winery. It's calm, still, silent, and the echoes sound strange as so much of the empty space is filled.

The first time I visited, it was this time of year. The wineries I'd visited before were grander in scale, the winemakers boasting armies of assistants and the very latest in technology. I never saw any of the dirty work. Equipment stored for the winter would not have been on the winery floor. Outside of harvest those places become marketing tools; used to show journalists, merchants and visitors the grand scale of investment; the cutting edge level of winemaking technology.

This small cave on the outskirts of Cosprons was not like that. It felt as though it worked for its wine. That afternoon Philippe climbed from barrel to barrel, wine-thief in hand, extracting samples and explaining each one with precision. I stood in rapt silence as he bounced about, knowing the order in the chaos of the resting wine. My French then was even worse than it is now, but somehow I felt I comprehended anyway. He spoke of each barrel's grape and soil and aspect to the sun and, importantly for him, its closeness to the sea. He apologised for the winery being in such a mess. At one point he climbed the ladder above the cool room to draw juice from a tiny cask, something folks in the whisky industry would probably call a quarter cask. What came from it was a deep, inky purple. A late-harvested Mourvèdre. I'd never tasted anything quite like it – somehow utterly pure and yet still earthy, dark and warming. He wasn't quite sure what he was going to do with it later. We sampled pre-blended wines, wines ready for bottling, whites and reds, sweeties and dry wines. Wine from the barrel is quite a sensory assault. It fills every corner of the mouth. If it's red, the tannins tend to be forward and rasping. If it's white it often smells sweet, but depending on where it is, it can be bracing and backwards and quite a shock to the system.

After the tasting we drove over to Philippe's home in Banyuls. The streets in the old part of town are maze-like. Philippe lives on the hill that forms the first part of the town, on a street so steep and narrow that I still don't quite know how anyone successfully navigates it. As well as his home, it's also the registered business address for the Coume del Mas. That has caused issues in the past, with lorry drivers carrying tons of equipment getting stuck along the narrow lanes, causing the sort of nigh-unsolvable traffic havoc perfectly suited to these small corners of the Mediterranean coast.

It was a simple lunch. A cousin had sent him some fresh perigord truffles and he made a fresh, fat-noodled pasta to shave them over. He opened an older bottle of Quadratur, the 2001. It was the third vintage he made. The dark berry fruit had given way to softer stone fruit and it tasted as though it had been soaking in Christmas spices. We chatted about the wine and life and the food was good. Philippe's house had the feel of somewhere built for the coziness; not too hot in the summer, but warm and comfy in the winter.

Wine folks often talk about what wines they like outside of their own area. That afternoon, I asked Philippe his favourites. He explained his love of the Côte Rôties from Jamet and the Sancerres of Gitton. I professed my love of Chambolle-Musigny (and Musigny) from Freddie Mugnier.

There was cheese to follow the pasta and truffles because it's France, and because it's France the cheese was delicious. The sort of cheese you keep picking at long after your stomach has told the brain it's full.

We had a wee coffee and then headed off and I felt I'd learned something, but I'm still not sure what. Regardless, I felt richer for it.

My first vintage, later that very year, I never noticed Philippe noting the particular parcels of vines being picked, or the filing in his head of each barrel and tank, commensurate to the truckload of grapes from whence they came. But he noted them all regardless, whether I noticed or not. I thought about that lunch, and the tour and tasting that preceded it, a lot that first harvest. It prepared me, in a way, for what was to come. Not the work, not by any stretch, but that one afternoon in January gave me a glimpse of everything a winemaker needs to be aware of to do their job.

WHISKY & CRACKPOTS

THE ROUSSILLON COULD BE CONSIDERED FULL
of crackpots. Mostly because it is. Up in the hills
are communes waiting for aliens. I've heard tales of
attempted murder and cuckolded husbands shooting up
restaurants in a rage, neither with any police involvement.
Winery sabotage is common and can be devastating, the most
frequent being quite simple. People break into a winery and
simply open the taps on the tanks, emptying out, in some
cases, several vintages worth of work. Again, the police don't
get involved. Often there are old grudges being settled and
the law doesn't want to get tangled in that.

It isn't all crime, UFOology and sabotage. In these remote
towns, parties can last for days and punishments/practical
jokes still include tarring and feathering. Beer is cheap in the
cafes and the surrounding quiet feels like a physical presence.
As though an invisible duvet has been set on top of the
valleys. There's something slightly muffled about it all. The
locals claim the *sangliers*, the wild boar, outnumber the
people, and they're probably right.

In Collioure, the Café Sola is shut for the month of January,
and then the Templiers closes for February. Most of the
restaurants are closed, too. Even many of the expats have disappeared northward, to home and the proper cold of winter.

Or maybe somewhere sunnier, in the tropics perhaps. But they're not here. The town moves at the same slow pace as the rest of the Roussillon during the winter. It's a good time for winemakers to travel and peddle their wares.

Andy and I were sat at my old black marble dining room table, which used to be his old black marble dining room table, drinking a 12-year-old cask strength Springbank and talking about art and science and wine. He added a dollop of water to his dram and said that more and more he feels winemaking is about science rather than art, and that when it all boils down to it, he's more a scientist than anything else. It was January in Scotland, and an east wind kicked battered the windows of my flat (which used to be his flat). We'd eaten a big meal with old friends, and there were several beers before and after that. My instinct was to disagree. So I did, at first without knowing why. Well, of course there's a huge amount of science involved, I said as I added my own dollop of water to my own dram. But there's science involved in everything. I didn't quite have a point just yet. But winemaking isn't just an annual experiment. There's no control group. Science guides winemaking in the same way that structural engineering guides architecture. It must be obeyed to achieve any manner of success, but what is memorable, what brings us back to a beautiful building or fantastic bottle of wine isn't the angle of incident or the grams per litre of residual sugar. We take in these things, we observe them and that is certainly part of what makes them so extraordinary, but that's not why we love and admire these things. All of that is filtered through the taste of the architect or winemaker. And their goal is not to make something that is scientifically perfect, or correct, but to make something pleasing to the eye and to the palate. I've had plenty of well-made wines that ticks all the boxes, but too often they come across as clinical, dull even. Architecture that places function over aesthetics can come across as boring or even hideous – just look at the some of Britain's offerings of the 50s and 60s; stab-your-eyes-out dreadful. In fact, the flat we sat in that night, battered by the winter wind, was a good example as any of a building that kept the wind out and the rain off but looked hideous in all its pebble-dashed glory.

Of course I didn't resort to such excessive metaphor usage when drinking whisky in the wee hours of the morning, but I did manage to boil it down to something along the lines of: you make wine that tastes good to you. That's the filter from which science becomes the artist's impression. Photosynthesis, geology, climate and biochemistry made the grapes, you turned the grapes into wine, but you turned the grapes into wine that you felt tasted the best, both of themselves and representing where they come from. Nobody else would have made the same wine. I wouldn't make the same wine. You may not think it's an art, or not feel you're an artist, but that doesn't really matter.

It's the luxury of the writer that in retrospect I can give myself such an unwavering argument. It's the one I believe, and that's the course I took on that cold Scottish evening. We continued to drink whisky and mulled taste and interpretation as much as possible. We agreed that much of winemaking is hard work and science. We topped up our glasses and further agreed that any winemaker calling themselves an artist was probably a bit of a wanker. I don't know if we agreed that the art in winemaking was the art in interpretation or not, or by that point we were discussing the beguiling toffee-coconut flavours that are Springbank's hallmark. The distiller's art is definitely in the blending. But like the winemaker, without great raw materials, there's no artwork. Picasso could pay a bill with a biro doodle on a serviette. There's no equivalent to that in winemaking.

And so the conversation went on until the thought of refilling the glasses was just that little bit too much. Winter's a good time to taste, drink and talk.

FRICTION BURNS &

OPTIMUS WINE

NOBODY LIKES BOTTLING. BY NECESSITY, IT'S the most automated thing we do, which means that quite a lot tends to go wrong. We don't have a bottling line, so we book the bottling truck. The bottling truck is used by almost all the independent vignerons in this neck of the woods. Only one independent winery that I know of has its own bottling line, and it's got its own problems.

A bottling line is modular. It comes in bits and pieces. There's the pump and filter, should you need to filter. We tend to filter based on the weather. A low-pressure system during bottling – a risk in the winter – can kick up the sediment in the bottom of the tank. We marry all of our wines in tank before bottling – it's just easier to bottle from them than from barrel. So if the weather's good, there will be little or no filtering. If the weather's bad, finer filters need to be used because there's bigger chunks of stuff floating about in the wine. After the pumps and filters comes the actual bottling module, where the liquid is piped into the glass vessels with a last little bit of sulphur. We use sulphur to stabilise our wines. I've mentioned it before. We don't apologise for this. The phrase: 'Contains sulphites' was chosen by a committee of American

politicians, including Strom Thurmond (a former segrega-
tionist), because it sounded scary, and they hoped it would
discourage drinking. Sulphites are a natural byproduct of
fermentation. Sulphur dioxide, when added to wine, acts
to perturb the effects of oxidation and prevent microbial
infection. That's a good thing. Loads of people think that
they're allergic to sulphites. Most of the time they're not.
They say it gives them a terrible hangover. I'm pretty sure
that's the booze. Unless they get a hangover from eating dried
apricots, or any other dried fruit, because there's far more
sulphur dioxide in those than there is in a bottle of wine.
Recently, there's been a movement promoting wines without
SO_2 added to them. This movement has caused a great deal
of controversy within the wine world, not least because the
tag that has been given to these wines is 'natural'. By calling a
certain group of wines 'natural' you're suggesting that any
wines made that don't fit in that group are somehow 'unnatu-
ral', which is nonsense. In any case, there has been many a
bust-up amongst wine folks with the pros and the antis all
making some interesting arguments. Me? I've had some good
wines without sulphur and I've had some abominations. I'm
not a big fan of dogma, so I probably fall somewhere in the
middle of the whole thing. I just want to help make great
wine. SO_2 helps that.

Anyway, I digress. Bottling.

I remember working in a wine shop in the lead up to the
Christmas rush, waiting with trepidation for pallet after pallet
of wines, whiskies and assorted other festive liquids. A fully
loaded pallet is, or should be, 56 cases. If the cases are six-
packs, then it's 112 cases per pallet. It was a small shop. It still
is, actually, and the sight of two pallets waiting to be brought

into its tight confines in short time could ruin an otherwise cheery morning. It often seemed an insurmountable task. A pallet was pretty much the largest measure of quantity we used. Occasionally there would be chat of shipping a whole container (which holds several pallets), but those chats were rare and inevitably ended with a shrug and a 'nah'.

When I worked as a sommelier, pallets of wine were rare and impractical. We received only two in my 14 months at the restaurant, of wine we shipped directly from France. It took some planning to clear room in the cellar, with various nooks and crannies excavated to stash a six-pack here and there.

The last few vintages I've worked in France, I've grown accustomed to the scale and volume of the wine we make. Fifty and sixty hectolitre tanks are filled over the course of a day or two of emptying comportes full of grapes into the de-stemmer, which leads to the pump, which leads to the tank. *Remontage* through fermentation, racking, daily density samples and tastings meant that those tanks were not idle once filled. We continue to interact with them throughout vinification. I grasped their size and dimensions within the boundaries of winemaking.

At the end of a day's work we'd often open a bottle of a previous vintage and maybe comment on how this year would be different. Would it be better? I understood, intellectually, that the liquid in the tank would someday be the liquid in the bottle. It's such an obvious thing, and yet there was a level of comprehension that was missing; a blank spot between the tank and the bottle.

The bottling truck arrived and in spite of the occasional technical difficulty the bottling line was set up. It was modular, with lots of bright stainless steel and more moving parts than seemed practical. Filters, pumps, conveyors, front labels, back labels, bottles, boxes, corks, caps, etc. all present in staggering quantities. I should point out that, sadly, a bottling truck is just a regular truck. It's not a specially modified truck with a bottling line built into it, like a giant transformer. That would be amazing. I was disappointed when I discovered the truth (as was one of my editors); that a bottling truck is just a truck with a load of modular bottling equipment in the back. All of it gets taken out and during bottling, it's just an empty truck. In my head, somewhere, maybe in southern Italy, someone has invented at transformer-like bottling truck. It would look vaguely steampunk, and be called Optimus Wine.

A bottle of wine is a small thing, perfectly formed for its task, yet the number of things that go into it to give that impression and provide that perfect form, is daunting. For me it was, anyway. Our job was to bottle around 15,000 litres – we needed to clear space in the tanks for this year's harvest.

My station on the line was boxes. I had to unfold cases and lay them on the line for my partner to fill with six bottles, then lay down the divider atop those so that the last six bottles could be placed on top of the divider. My partner then folded the case shut and pushed it through for it to be sealed, coded and loaded onto a pallet. We switched places for the last tank, with me handling the bottles. None of this occurred at a leisurely pace. We packed three cases a minute, thus filling a whole pallet in less than 20 minutes. Before my very eyes the tanks I knew only in and of themselves were emptying into bottles and the scale took me aback. Just one of those 60 hecto tanks equalled 8,000 bottles of wine. That's almost 12 pallets worth. Mas Cristine is not a huge winery. A 15,000 litre bottling line in the Roussillon is at best small-to-medium in terms of volume. And yet for this former wine merchant, the one who would sigh in exasperation when a delivery driver showed up outside the shop with two pallets, to bottle and box over 20 pallets worth of wine in the space of a day and a half seemed extraordinary.

After that last day of bottling we went home and, as usual, cracked open a bottle of something. I brushed the label with my thumb and traced the seam of the glass up to the foil cap. The cork removed, I rolled it over in my fingers and squeezed it, feeling it give slightly. I nosed my glass, looked again at the label and thought that a bottle of wine is a small thing.

After the liquid goes in the bottle, the cork (*bouchon*) gets stuffed in and then the foil and then the real bastard bit of the whole thing, the labels. We use both front and back labels, and they have to be calibrated so that they are precisely centred on each other. Why is that a big deal? It isn't, not really, because it's the wine inside the bottle that's the important thing. But at the same time, if you can't get the labels straight on the bottle, then how can you be trusted with the wine on the inside? It's one of those stupid little things that seems like it shouldn't make a difference but does. If you're an average punter gazing upon the shelves in your local independent wine merchant and you stumble upon a label that looks like it was stuck on by someone who didn't give a shit, all things being equal, you wouldn't buy that wine. I wouldn't blame you – I probably wouldn't buy those lazy assholes' wine either.

So we recalibrate. We have empty, dummy bottles for such things. It involves running the empty bottle through a number of times whilst fiddling with the settings until once again the front and back labels are in sync. Then you repeat a couple of times just to make sure. Then you start the whole thing again and hope it works.

The labels come on huge rolls with thousands upon thousands of labels. I'm always kind of curious how long they would be if you unravelled them. I could work it out, but I'm happy just to remain curious, rather than spout some improbable distance like those guys who take great joy in telling you that your lungs would cover a tennis court if fully unfolded.

Finally, sealed, full and labelled, the bottles come out on a conveyor belt and need to be boxed. Boxing should be a two-man job, though quite frequently it's one man. The boxes are all flat-packed, and so have to be unfolded quite quickly. If you're in the zone, you're dealing with bottles pretty much as they come out and you can box up about four cases of 12 a minute. You then push the box through this machine that both seals it with tape and prints the cuvée on the side of the box.

The cases are then stacked on a pallet until there are 56 of them, at which point the pallet is wrapped in loads of giant cling film which is then sealed, much to my initial horror and amusement, by a massive flaming torch that shrinks the film tight around the cases, holding them fast atop the pallet for whatever future they may have. Some will go to the States (those ones have special labels on the back, complete with Surgeon General's warnings and that sort of thing).

Bottling is kind of like everything else around here. You do it until it's done. You do it as the friction burns sear into your fingers as you flip bottles by their necks into the boxes, trying to keep up with the machines around you. You only have the bottling truck for the day, and so all the wine you're planning on putting into bottle has to be put into bottle there and then. Breakages, delays, re-calibrating the labels (the latter has to be done a lot) all stretch the day out into evening, but you still don't leave until the tanks are empty and the bottles are full.

GINS & TONIC

S AP RISING AND BUD BREAK. SPRING WAKES UP
the vines and the towns they surround. The expats slowly
return. The rains come, and many of the streets in
Collioure turn briefly into rivers. The change in the vines is
the best. They slowly shed their skeletal look as the buds
break; the leaves begin to open and spread out to face the sun.
The hills and mountains transform slowly from greyscale to
technicolour. It's not quite like in the *Wizard of Oz*, when
Dorothy opens the door of her Kansas farmhouse to a sudden
flood of colour, but it's not far off.

All thoughts of the cold and the dank quickly evaporate.
Winter doesn't linger in the memory long in warm places.
Late in the winter and early in the spring, the vines get
ploughed. We have a horse for this, a big old shire horse
named Titan who used to plough the vines at some of
Burgundy's finest *domaines*. Some of the vines in Banyuls are
too steep for Titan; these will be done by hand.

People return to Collioure and Banyuls and Argelès bit
by bit. Holiday-goers from far afield and expats; this is very
much an expat time of year, as it precedes the hordes that
arrive in July and August when the French schools are out
and, apparently, nobody in France has to work. And as these
people arrive, we're bottling new wines for them to drink.

This is when the first of our wines from the previous harvest, only about eight months ago, are bottled and ready for sale. Wine just bottled can be a little different from what you're used to, especially when you leave it as much to its own devices as you possibly can. With our whites, this is the freshest they will be, some of them, like the Mas Cristine Blanc, will even feel as though there's a hint of effervescence – there isn't, but it will feel like it. The rosés will be sharp and clean and hint at strawberries and cranberries. The reds will be crunchy and, if I'm lucky, the Mas Cristine Rouge will smell just like the back of Julien's pickup when it's loaded with grapes to be thrown into the de-stemmer, wild red fruits, honeysuckle and a bit of dust kicked up on a dry sunny day. We don't make enough white. It's in demand, but there just aren't enough vineyards planted with white varieties to meet that demand. New plantings take time, and when there are people wanting something that you can't give them, that time seems eternal. Juggling allocations for customers gets more difficult for Andy and Philippe every year. By the time the new vintage is bottled and ready to go, all of our best customers have been waiting for at least a month or two for stock. Anyone who waits too long to confirm an order will have their wines allocated to someone more decisive.

Recently, Andy managed to get our basic rosé, the Tramontane Rosé, on the list at the Templiers in Collioure as their house pink by the bottle, so the second rosé up the ladder. Their house pouring rosé is a rather tasty bag-in-box that they sell for about six Euros a half-litre pichet. Anyway, this was quite a coup. Most of the bars in town make do with the co-op offerings. Andy reserved 600 bottles for them and they went through it in a month. I don't think even they knew how popular it was going to be. It's a good wine, but being a rosé, and the second cheapest rosé probably helped it more so (studies show that the second cheapest wine on a wine list can often prove to be the most popular, as folks want a bargain, but don't want to seem too miserly). In any case, they went through their allocation for the year in about a month. So we had to put a bit more aside for them this year.

Along with the Café Sola, the Templiers forms the binary system around which most of the debauchery and drunkenness in Collioure revolves. It's a hotel, restaurant and bar owned by a local family that have been collecting art for a century or so. Behind the bar is a photo of Picasso, signed with a doodle, stood next to the grand or great-grandfather of the current generation of owners. Every inch of wall space is covered in paintings, all of them framed in heavy, gilded, ornate frames, the likes of which are probably more expensive than some of the art they hold now. They don't show off their good stuff anymore. Too many priceless canvases disappeared with the odd unscrupulous punter. Picassos probably sit at the top of the tier, but there are others, such as Matisse, now all locked safe elsewhere. Rumour has it that when the Templiers has a bad year, when the wolves are closing in and bills need to be paid, the family will release a painting for auction to get them through. The work that hangs now, not just in the bar but throughout the hotel, is fine. It's dingy and thickly oiled, interesting in and of itself as it charts the local art that didn't achieve fame. A chronicle of also-rans and wannabes. You wouldn't find a collection like this anywhere else, because no one would collect it. Some of them are lovely, in fact. It's like a Battersea Dog's Home for art. I've not known a museum to specialise in the obscure, but the idea has merit. The potential curator could go to the Templiers to see how it's done. Of course, if they got stuck into the G&Ts

expertly crafted by the Brazilian barman, they might find themselves in a bit of trouble.

No one around here uses measures when they make drinks. They just free pour. Now, in some places, this means that you still get about the same as you would in a bar in the UK. Not so at the Templiers (nor in the Petit Café, but that's another place and another tale).

Sometimes after a day in the winery the pain's a bit too much for beer alone, and you need a proper muscle relaxant. The sort of thing that harkens back to the martinis made in the days of *Mad Men* – an immediate de-stresser, so laden with booze that it bypasses the brain and loosens everything else before you even realise it. That's what the Brazilian's gin and tonics do. They come in narrow, tall glasses, loaded with ice. He holds the gin upside down for almost a five-count, until there's barely more than an inch left between the top of the liquid and the rim of the glass. If you'd not seen him pre-pare it thus far, you might think the drink was finished. It looks finished. You might think the tonic was just a bit flat. But no. There's a whole 3/4s of an inch of tonic to add, and then it's done. The tonic may still be a bit flat. It's this gin and tonic that proves the essentialness of a swizzle stick. Without it, you'd sip away the tonic in one gulp and be left nearly choking on a tall gin on the rocks. Swizzle away, blend that splash into the ocean of gin and marvel how incredibly drink-able it all becomes. Oh, sure, there's a bitter edge here and there, but before you know it, you'll be feeling much better than you were. During harvest, we usually stick to just the one gin. It does the job. After that; beer.

In the spring, however, among friends and with the table covered in beers of various sizes, the odd carafe and pichet of wine, perhaps a glass or two of pastis with the requisite pitcher of tap water alongside and maybe a couple of glasses of Banyuls for apéro, sometimes another gin and tonic hits the spot. After two, you've got to watch yourself, because it's quite likely that the reflexive ability to assess your own fitness for function disappeared in those last few sips. If the conversation and company is good, as it usually is around these parts, then you could find yourself lost to the night, working your way through each of the drinks listed above. Possibly falling in the sea or, in a reckless state of abandon, phoning pretty much the only taxi in town and demanding he drive you to the casino or, worse, La Jonquera, the Spanish border town riddled with hookers who've been known to thieve card details and run up a several thousand pound tab in the course of only a few hours.

I'm not speaking from direct experience of the latter. Honest.

Good company on these evenings involves a mixture of local and expat colour. Earlier in the evening, Petit Louis may be about. Petit Louis is probably not quite five feet tall and as far as I can remember has had about three 90th birthday parties in the last five or so years. So I'll just assume he's over 90. He used to be a fisherman, and now he makes small model fishing boats that he charges a ridiculous amount for. His workshop and gallery sit just up the winding road from Andy and Kirsten's flat. Kirsten's portait of Petit Louis, next to a gutted fish that I think is a mackerel but may well be something else has become her calling card for the town, as she captured him perfectly. Age has carved deep folds into his face, which appears fixed in various forms of smile and laughter. He looks sort of like a happy bloodhound. I've never seen him in anything other than blue denim, both in terms of shirt and trousers, no matter how much the sun is beating down. Petit Louis knows everyone. His walk from the workshop to the Sola or the Templiers tends to be a walk of smiles, greetings, handshakes and the traditional kisses on both cheeks for the ladies. He still loves the ladies, and is quite the flirt.

The only one who doesn't say hi to Petit Louis is Max. I'm not sure what Max did in his professional life. He's younger than Petit Louis, and unsurprisingly taller. He too knows pretty much everyone in town and flirts relentlessly with the ladies. Perfectly white hair framed by dark but slightly salty arched eyebrows, Max must be somewhere in his sixties, but again, I'm not quite sure. If they're both out, quite often one will be at the Sola and the other at the Templiers. The division runs deep, and apparently there's a woman and a trip to Paris and the root of it all, but that's just hearsay.

One particular April evening, I sipped from a glass of rosé at the Templiers and kept up with the conversation. It was quite a few expats that evening, most of them just down and still a bit pale from the winter and sunless spring. I got chatting to a retired Cornishman. He and his wife have a place down here. He didn't seem to like it very much. He had the grumpy demeanour of someone who'd become a bit bored of retired life and was slowly beginning to think the world around him was pretty stupid, and that he must be pretty stupid to be still putting up with it after all these years. But still, quite fun to chat with. He drank red wine, but didn't like to spend too much on it. He did like the wine down here. He liked the wine that we made, as it happens. 'I like the big stuff' he said, sounding every bit the west countryman, even though his work had taken him all over the world. He could have offered to sell me a litre of farmer's scrumpy and I wouldn't have flinched. I supped my beer and he drank his wine and he asked what I did and I told him I made and sold wine and he told me he was retired but used to be a businessman.

'And what business was that?' I asked

'Oh, I was an arms dealer,' was the reply. I didn't comically choke on my pint, but in my head I did. The idea of this softly spoken West Country accent offering fleets of fighter jets and lorry-loads of M-16s rather than a litre of dodgy cider knocked me down a peg or two, I must admit. I got the impression he was quite high up in his former employment and was later told that he brokered meetings between defence ministers and various heads of government and state. At the time, however, he was just a bloke in the Templiers on a warm April evening sipping on a glass of red and talking about how he loathed the French.

'Well, I don't really loathe them, you see, I just can't be bothered to speak the language.'

I nodded with understanding and lamented that I didn't speak better French, and if I could, I may well have moved here by now.

'Oh, I wouldn't bother if I were you. What's the point in learning French? It's a dead language. As dead as a dodo. French, German, Italian, all of 'em. Pointless. All dead soon enough.'

This was another comedy spitting-my-pint out moment, but instead I swallowed and chuckled. It was pretty funny.

'As far as I'm concerned, it's just English, Spanish and Chinese that folks should bother learning these days. No bloody point in learning any others. They'll be nothing but historical footnotes. Fifty; hundred years from now, it'll just be English, Spanish and Chinese. And Spanish'll be lucky. So I refuse to speak French. And I'm too old and not bothered to learn a new language now, anyway.'

I nodded and told him I could see what he meant. And I could, I suppose. It was one of those sweeping statements said by someone with such conviction and simple logic that getting into an argument would have been pointless. I didn't bring up that French was important for me now, and that in trying to understand a winemaker's nuanced instructions, pointing out the potential extinction of their mother tongue as a justification for my ignorance would go down about as well as pissing in a fermentation vat.

He comes down here because his wife likes it. He gets along ok, he supposes, but doesn't really get into it as much as some of the others do. It's fun to think of him as merely a character. Broken veins stretch across his cheeks and nose, his eyes are watery. The glass of red he's drinking is not his first, nor will it be his last. He doesn't give a shit what I think, and I can't be bothered to challenge his dismal view of things, hence my nodding accompanied by just the odd protestation that I like it here. He doesn't really care. I'm getting that way, on occasion, where everyone is of course entitled to their opinion, but I reserve the right to not give a shit what it is.

I've been an expat for more than half my life. I moved away from the city and country I was born in in 1989 and, aside from two years at boarding school in the mid-90s, have lived elsewhere ever since. It's something I've always been aware of. I like it, because it means that I can feel very quickly at home pretty much anywhere. I feel at home in Collioure as much as I do in Boston, London or St Andrews. But I never really used to hang out in packs of like-folks. My parents had fellow expat friends and whatnot, but for the most part, I'd say we were fairly integrated. My friends were mostly Londoners, and when I went to university, they were from all over the place: Scotland, England, the States, Norway, Switzerland, Nepal, wherever. I even knew a guy from the Faro Islands. He loved Australian Shiraz.

But the point is, I never really experienced the idea of an expat community until I saw it in Collioure. I saw mention of it, obviously, but most of my thoughts and images were formed by people like Hemingway, Orwell and Fitzgerald. The idea of the young and aspiring seeking out their place in the world, adventuring, making art, living for the moment so much as to seem nihilistic. Tangoing, eating and drinking and fucking; moveable-feasting; being both of the places they went and yet utterly separate. Valuing that dichotomy above all; the idea that they could enjoy the riches of a place while still having a home to go back to. Behaving, for the most part, appallingly, because they could get away with it. Anything they did wouldn't matter at all, because any consequences would be so far away from home, away from those you cared about or would be embarrassed by your behaviour. I read *The Sun Also Rises* my senior year in high school. None of the class were really ready for that sort of selfish decadence in the form of fiction. We balked at the racism, political incorrectness and general odiousness of everyone involved. I revisited it a couple of years ago and understood it far better. I even liked it as a novel, in spite of the remaining irredeemability of the characters.

The expats in Collioure are like those Hemingway characters except a little more likeable and a little older. They eat out and drink at lunchtime, which often leads to eating out and drinking at dinner time as well. Often the conversation at lunch will be where to go for dinner. They fit no simple category; some are retired arms dealers, some are married, some are divorced, some are lovers, most drink too much (but who am I to talk), they party and drink and fuck and do drugs and some speak better French than others. There's nothing really predictable about them. I say 'them' as though they were a single entity; they aren't, not really. There are overlapping groups and some who quite purposely choose to keep to themselves. But the appearance is that of unity. Everyone tends to say hello in the Café Sola or the Templiers. Often tables will be pulled together and another carafe of wine bought. At this time of year, the air is fresh and the wine is fresh. All along the coast and throughout France, as green returns to the vines; bars, cafes and restaurants begin to serve the newly bottled fruits of the previous autumn. Sat in front of the Café Sola, you'll hear a few more English voices as they sup their small goblets of fresh rosé poured from a pichet. Donald might be there, the formidable Scottish hotelier whose knowledge of those here from elsewhere is peerless. His cane-bearing hand rises constantly in greeting, as he knows or at least recognises most of the people who pass by. He's quick to offer a drink and, if he's just arrived from Scotland, there will no doubt be plentiful smoked salmon, and Stornoway Black Pudding (which he prefers to the local *boudin noir*) in tow. He owns The George in Inveraray, a coaching inn that's been in the family for five or six generations. His sons have the running of it now. Stay there if you can, or if you're just passing through, stop for the mussels. They're the best I've eaten, and would turn many a Belgian green with envy.

Around Donald revolves much of the expat world in Collioure. Those overlapping groups all tend to overlap in his vicinity. He'll often suggest popping over to Spain for long Sunday lunches that stretch into dinner and sometimes even lunch the following day. He knows seemingly everyone, local and visitor. He introduces himself if he doesn't. My first introduction to him was at Andy and Kirsten's wedding, where he instructed me to rent a kilt on Max's behalf. I don't think

Max really believed Donald was going to go through with it, and to be honest, I was a little hesitant to arrange for a kilt on someone's behalf sight unseen. There are a lot of very particular measurements that go into getting a kilt right. I didn't want to bring an outfit 1,000 miles for it not to fit. When I spoke to Donald on the phone he said not to worry. And I shouldn't have. Max looked great in a kilt, and even managed not to upend himself after the several gallons of Banyuls consumed at the wedding.

Donald tends to be the observer and sometimes instigator of the outrageous, but very rarely the perpetrator. Instead he'll regale those at the table of the various incidences of the night before, often with a bit of a twinkle in his eye and the odd sigh of a hangover, and very little damage done to or by his good self.

An afternoon that Donald holds court is one that can last far longer than intended. He often starts by offering you a glass of the splendid red he's drinking, but oh dear, there's only a drop or two left in the bottle. And so another is ordered and depending on how many folks are there, quickly put to rest by just the filling of the surrounding glasses. And so a scant few sips after they've been raised, they must be filled again. And so another bottle will arrive and this lasts a little longer, as pleasantries have been exchanged and the chat becomes relaxed and constant with problems of both the world and closer to home given the once over before moving back towards the gossip of the town and the chat amongst the locals. This conversation will often include recently dined at restaurants and/or the drunken antics of the evening before. As soon as food is brought up and the glasses are empty another bottle is ordered and discussion moves towards what people's dinner plans are. Some folks may be intending to go home for a meal and some may have a table booked locally. By the time the third bottle sits in its dregs and a round of beers is ordered (that fantastic new wine might not have been that fantastic after all) a restaurant's been mentioned that no one's been to recently, or that is under new management or ownership. Questions about how solid everyone's former plans are. Who wants to cook at this hour? Could we get another wee dish of olives and peanuts please? Oh, and a few more beers – oh? You want wine? Three beers and a bottle of wine then, please. Well do you think they'll have a table for nine on a night like this? There's only one way to find out.

And I think that's what's called a moveable feast.

Collioure is split in two by a rather large fortification set into a natural hilly outcrop. To travel from one half of the city to the other, you can walk along the stony walkway that surrounds the fort, along the water, passing the odd artist, street musician and ticket tout for day-sailing on the Med. The art ranges from middling to terrible. There are spots where you can see the masonry of the fort sat square on the bedrock. Doubtless there will be a few fisherman too, their rods leant against a rock or gripped lazily. I think the fishing is more important than the idea of catching anything. The water's always crystal clear – dark reefs cross the white pebble and stone sea floor like tiger stripes. In the spring there's a brightness to the light and a coolness in the air that makes the clearness of the water that much sharper. The coolness sits behind the ever-present breeze, a reminder of the snows from the mountains, and the winter not long past.

Or you can walk up the hill, behind the fort, to the mini roundabout. You pass at least one tasting room and Olivier Bajard's remarkable confectioners. At the top of the hill is an improbable Renault garage and petrol station. Further up past the roundabout is the big Anchois Roque shop, cannery and tasting area, where you can learn pretty much everything you want to about Collioure's famous anchovies. Whether they tell you that they're no longer from the Med, that they're only canned here, depends on how honest they're feeling that day. I believe they all come from South American waters now, what with the sea here about quite empty.

It's a nicer walk up the hill in the spring than it is in the summer. In the summer there's an endless queue of cars seeking their way towards one of the rare parking spots in the town. The odd honk of a horn and the craning necks of drivers looking for a glimmer of a space wherever they may be. Any movement in their periphery could be a car exiting the perfect spot. It isn't. But it could be.

By the mini roundabout, you turn left and start walking down the hill, towards the other half of town. This is the side that rises up again on the other side of the beach and then just sort of turns into Port-Vendres. There's a good beach here, and a café that serves pizzas. Children play on the playground and there's even a carousel. Along this stretch is the scuba school and paddle boat hire. The Les Voiles café sits terraced above the water and is a good, but pricey, spot for lunch. The best place to eat in this part of town, however, is the L'Arbre d'Voyageur. A tiny place in a small square across the street from the beach, there's barely room for inside seating. There's a bar and stools, but behind the bar is the kitchen. This is where Michel makes his remarkable food.

Traditional Catalan food is fantastic, and there's superb produce in the region. Their particular brand of tapas is fresh and influenced very much by both the sea and the moun-tains. That said, there's a lot of mediocre dining in Collioure.

Why? Because they can get away with it. Thronging with tourists for several months of the year, a lot of restaurants and cafés punt out any old rubbish, charge too much for it and get away with it. I can think of three or four places whose menus are basically interchangeable. It's a real shame. There should be dozens of great restaurants here, not just a handful.

Michel doesn't do the traditional Catalan thing. There's enough of it kicking about. Instead, Michel lets the exotic notes of North Africa, India and Thailand influence his food, and makes a remarkable selection of fresh and exotic curries, steak tartar, but set in a thai salad, Moroccan lamb and his unique take on Rogan Josh. He makes everything from scratch. It's the sort of food you keep eating long after you're full, just because it's so compelling bite after bite.

Michel himself isn't a chef by training, and his fame in Collioure predates his cooking. Once upon a time he ran the Piano Bar, a remarkable little bar built into some of the oldest parts of Collioure. It didn't have a piano – it still doesn't, in fact – which is why it was called the Piano Bar. Michel's CD collection numbers in the thousands, and the Piano Bar used to jump to jazz, blues, African, all sorts of perfectly chosen tracks that kept the night going. It felt like a cave, seemingly carved out of a mediaeval stone wall. Only room for one behind the bar, Michel's thing was world beers, and he had a small but perfectly formed selection. After Andy's wedding, this is where the survivors met for a post revelry livener.

Sadly, Michel was just a little bit too much fun to run a pub in town, and he lost his lease on the Piano Bar. It's still there, but rather soulless. We don't drink there anymore. I don't even know if the people that run it know why it's called the Piano Bar.

It would be hard to look more French than Michel. Tall

and slight, with a weathered face and gestures with his arms while speaking that are at once energetic and lackadaisical. Rarely is there not a cigarette hanging from his mouth (usually just when he's cooking). He drives a moped and can sometimes nap so late that the restaurant doesn't open for dinner until a half hour after you were hungry. One vintage Andy had to go to Paris for a sales meeting and I was left to run Mas Cristine for a couple of days. Kirsten was heavily pregnant with Angus, and fairly grumpy. And so when I finished in the winery, I would head back to the flat, shower and change and then slip back out to Michel's, order a couple of beers or a pichet of wine, and sit out at a table for one. I'd just ask him what was best that night. It was quiet and cool and I could hear the sea from across the street. His daughter would run around playing until her mom would grow weary of the hyperactivity and rein her in. At a break in cooking, Michel would pop out for a cigarette and sit with me, sipping a beer. His English is better than my French, and he would ask how it was all going with harvest. The food was so good, so utterly nourishing at that point of exhaustion.

L'Arbre won't be open on a spring afternoon, but it's fun to see if Michel's moped is there, just to see if he's prepping in the kitchen early or napping away. If he's prepping he might get some bookings for the evening, as the smell that comes as he browns and sweats spices over the cooker acts as quite the bait for many a curious diner.

This end of town is also where the Cave Dominicain sits, the co-op in town. Above that is the local art museum, which I've never seen open, and the hillside gardens that lead to what is now an ornamental moulin – a windmill that stands above the town. If you follow the road that grabs the side of the hill, it will bring you up to the Neptune, which used to be the only Michelin Star restaurant in town. It was dining there many years ago that Andy first tasted Philippe's wines. It's lost its star, but the food's still good, if a little pricey. It's up on the hill over the harbour, though, and the views are spectacular.

Further up the hill are hotels built into the cliffside overlooking the water. And so it goes until it's not Collioure anymore but Port-Vendres. A large Lidl sits on the border between the two towns.

Port-Vendres has a good wine shop but I've not really eaten much there. A rash of food poisonings from a pizza place on the harbour one January visit has left me a little lacking in enthusiasm for revisiting the cuisine.

A few years ago, Andy, Philippe and Julien invited a bunch of customers to Mas Cristine for a spring party, to celebrate not only the new vintage, but the fifth anniversary of Philippe and Julien's partnership in the estate (Andy joined the group a year after they took it over). A bit strange, really, to invite folks to Mas Cristine, as it's one of the most unappealing wineries in the known universe. But they'd secured a deal with the family that actually owns the house, Mas Cristine. The house is beautiful. A classic French farmhouse guarded from peeking eyes by a perfect row of poplars and set up in the hills between Argelès and Collioure. It looks out towards the sea, and is set in the vines from which we make the wine that bears its name. To the sides and behind it rise the foothills of the mountains, and at this time of year, with the leaves all back and the frequency of the rains, there's a remarkable sense of *life* surrounding you. You can almost hear the cork forest growing, the vines stretching to get more of the sun and perhaps even the grunt of the occasional boar from just beyond the tree line. Those hills always feel like the mountains of South/Central America and there is a sense of the tropical. It's like a rain forest, but without quite so much rain.

The deal that Julien and Philippe struck was permission to use the front garden and the old front garage in order to host this big bash. Sometimes the wine trade is just about drinking loads of lovely wine and having a great party. Old French garages do not stand with other garages of the world. They're bigger, for one, and their dimensions suggest that their entire purpose was to make wine. In this case, it was very likely that this large space made the very first vintages of wine that bore the name 'Mas Cristine' decades, maybe a century and more, ago. It's a combination of excitement and sadness that comes with that realisation. Excitement that, for the first time, we get to hang out at this place and pretend it's our own and be in the very room that saw the wine being made all those years ago. But also sadness that it's different now. The family who own the house use it rarely. From what I understand, they're also in the wine world, but on a much grander scale than us. I kind of feel this oversized garage should still be used to make wine, rather than as a shed that just makes the small amount stored in it look even smaller because it's so big in the first place. The house is all properly faced on the outside, it's only in the garage that you see the large wooden beams that provide the support and structure to the building. I reach out and touch them. I do that sometimes. I like touching old things, be it stone or wood. Just to get some sort of sense of how it feels. I know there's no supernatural connection or anything like that, but there doesn't have to be. The sensation of touch in itself can be moving enough as it is.

We set up two marquees on the perfectly manicured front lawn and secured them against the wind. The Tramontane was predicted in force for both days of the party, and so we wanted to make sure that they didn't go anywhere. It's the sort of precaution I expected more in Scotland. Having to deal with it under the beating sun in semi-paradise seemed somewhat awry. On further examination though, the sun wasn't beating that hard, and there appeared to be some very large clouds rolling in off the mountains.

We set out a lot of wine. Most of our best customers were showing up, and as it was in part an anniversary, Philippe brought out some of the small amounts of library stock he'd hidden over the years, including a bottle of the first Coume del Mas wine ever, a blend that would become, eventually, Quadratur. There was also some Mas Cristine Blanc from 2006, his first vintage, and samples from barrel of both Grand Cru and Rancio styles of Banyuls that have still not been bottled, because Philippe doesn't think they're quite ready yet.

Library stock is a term used in the wine world for bottles kept back from sale each vintage by the winery for the purposes of storing in ideal conditions. Some wineries have library stock numbering in the millions of bottles and spanning two or three centuries. These will be opened rarely, on special occasions, by winemakers and château owners to chart the progress of a wine and study the effects of time, or to compare how two vintages from similar climatic conditions might age. Sometimes they just open them because they can. Who can blame them? That's probably what I would do.

Library wines are usually stored unlabelled, with their only identifying mark being that of the un-foiled cork, bearing both the name of the cuvée and the year of the vintage. This allows them to be freshly labelled when released for whatever the occasion may be. It can be somewhat bizarre; an ancient bottle and cork adorned by a fresh-from-the-printer label. Like a granny dressed as Lady Gaga.

Sadly, we don't make enough wine for such testaments to posterity. It would be lovely to have a cellar built under the winery at Coume del Mas, filled with all the vintages Philippe has ever made both there and at Mas Cristine. Instead we rely on a few odd bottles here and there that Philippe has hidden away somewhere special. I can only assume he keeps them at home, as Coume del Mas is so open plan, there aren't any nooks or even crannies to slip a few dozen bottles of wine in. And we're still a young company. We make wine to sell, and need to realise as much from that as we can to keep going for the next year. It's a bit too much of a luxury to sit on it for a big party.

There were magnums of Folio and Schistes and I was struck by a pang of selfishness. Who needs guests or customers, anyway? Brushing aside my urge to hide the good stuff for myself, I managed to take the tasting quite seriously. I sampled every single wine, swirled and spat, and noted absolutely everything. Customers from all over France came, including a wine merchant from Paris whose cellars go down into what were, originally, catacombs. The wines get older the deeper you descend through the cellars, with the most ancient bottles resting in the lowest levels of the catacombs. Andy described it like something out of Indiana Jones. I still have the gentleman's business card (somewhere). I very much want to go to that shop, though fear that my meagre bank balance would not survive the trip.

Tray after tray of tapas came out. Loaf after loaf of fresh bread cut into slices and served rubbed with a mixture of ripe tomato and garlic that constitutes one of Catalonia's signature dishes. People fed and drank. The local wine merchants, wise to the gems on offer at the tasting tables, would grab something particularly rare for their own benefit. This gave rise to one of the afternoon's more childish but good-humoured pursuits. I'd not tried the Grand Cru Banyuls yet – they got to it before me. And so it became a bit of a race, to see who could get to the rarest bottle and serve themselves the largest 'sample'. I was fortunate as I was playing with house money, as it were. Some more samples of the older Banyuls, both the Grand Cru and the Rancio, appeared and I helped myself, raising two glasses in their direction with a smile. Then Philippe handed me a bottle of his first ever vintage and an experimental 'super' cuvée that he'd put in barrel one year and totally forgotten about – essentially a Quadratur with an extra year blended in oak. Soft and silky. I didn't actually open those, to be honest. They found their way into my rucksack and are now sleeping quite happily in a cellar in Scotland.

Sipping the two older Banyuls quickly erased the silliness of sneaking about trying to get my hands on this and that before the merchants did. They put a pin in the map of my mind, nailed me to that lawn in front of Mas Cristine as I stood between the two marquees. Intense flavours expressed on the palate with such beauty that the rest of the wine that day, for the most part, has faded into shadow. I took my time with them; wandered down to the end of the lawn by the poplars and tried to take everything in from both the glasses and my surroundings. The patchwork of sunlight and cloud cover, the sound of the strong breeze in the trees, the clanging of the weighted tarpaulin of the marquees against the tentpoles. I quite often seek my own space in such big gatherings, but this time I needed it. The wines were close to perfect expressions of their style. I could have spent the rest of the afternoon just sipping those two wines and staring out towards the sea through the poplar trees. But lunch was ready.

It was here that I first met hippy Kris and we got into our

first discussion regarding the pros and cons of 'natural' wine-making, biodynamics, organic viticulture and sustainable winemaking. Kris is very pro all of those things. I wouldn't call him hippy Kris if he wasn't. I should mention that I'm not necessarily against any of those things myself, but I do like winding up folks carrying a little too much dogma about with them, and Kris certainly qualified. So we debated and argued and went back and forth about adding sulphur and mystical 'energies' in certain soils. At this point, I was unaware that it was his strange guano fertiliser cocktail that had spilled in the Mighty Clio, rendering it close to toxic. A wine merchant from London was sat next to us and extraordinarily curious about Kris' theories. My sparring partner preferred evangelising to debate and so shifted his attention from me to the interested onlooker.

And so I grabbed my glass and headed back towards the tasting marquee in good spirits, though wanting to revisit some of the wines I'd tried earlier. Try as I might, I couldn't repeat the moment with the two Banyuls. They were every bit as good the second time around, but there was no nailing to the spot or pins in maps. Instead there was the urge to start tidying up and clear everything away for the day. The paper tablecloths were tattered and stained, and many of the samples were empty. I put my glass down and started to help with the clear up.

In the evening after the party, a bunch of us, those that had travelled the furthest, either from Britain or Paris, went to Masashi's for dinner.

Lijima Masashi, as his name suggests, is Japanese. He's a chef. He came to France to train at the highest level and now has a restaurant of his own, Le 5ème Péché. He makes French/Japanese fusion cuisine that is the opposite of how wanky that sounds. In fact, it's deceptively simple how good his food is. Expressive, pure flavours that come from delicate treatment of only the very finest ingredients. The restaurant is tiny (though not as small as Michel's), located on the Rue de la Fraternité, one of the tiny, narrow lanes in the old town of Collioure that is almost entirely populated by funky little art galleries. In that sense, Masashi is well-situated. His food frequently reaches artistic levels of creativity and Masashi himself kind of wants to be a rock star. He plays guitar, and in the afternoon between lunch service and dinner, you can frequently hear him blasting out hard rock from his kitchen while he gets his *mise en place* sorted for the evening. His chef hat hides a mane of hair that swooshes perfectly when he's playing AC/DC covers in the garage of his house on one of the hills behind Port-Vendres. His wine list is good and he shows quite a few of the region's 'natural' wine selection. Some of these are fantastic, like the Bruno Duchêne Collioure Rouge. And some of them leave a bit to be desired. We once opened a bottle, quite an expensive one at that, that was re-fermenting and tasted far more of cider than it did wine.

Philippe once again produced, seemingly from thin air, some old magnums of both Quadratur and Abysses, his two top reds, from an exceptional year, the 2005 vintage. The wine showed brilliantly. After the meal, a fair few of us decamped to the Templiers for a G&T or two.

The following day, back at Mas Cristine, Julien had arranged for three whole lambs to be cooked on rotisserie spits, over a mixture of charcoal and old grape vines. It was a stark contrast to the laser-like precision of the meal before, but every bit as toothsome. The lamb was dripping with flavour, served with large batches of couscous, spiced up with

livid, fiery harissa. The wine cooled down the heat, thankfully, and stood up to the spice. It was messy and beautiful.

So it was a toss-up, between the two, which food was better.
Masashi's pristine cuisine the night before or the lamb cooked
on spits that second day of the party. It's good that no one was
forced to choose between the two. And it was a brilliant way
to kick off the growing season.

TORN LIGAMENTS &
VINTAGE HANDS

SPRING IS NOT ONLY ABOUT PARTYING. WITH the vines awake, there is much to do. Throughout the winter, time in the vineyards is mostly maintenance and pruning. Once the buds break and the sap is rising, viticulture becomes very much a mixture of both farming and gardening. As soon as the vines have leaves again, they have to be protected. Even organic and biodynamic viticulture allows for the use of what's called Bordeaux Mixture, a very simple solution of copper and sulphur that helps keep rot away and reduce the threat of nasty things like oidium. Spraying Bordeaux Mixture takes some time. You should work in teams of two – on the terrain that we work, lugging a massive tank full of liquid on your back is ridiculously hazardous.

One spring, José went out to do a quick bit of spraying on his own. Normally, his son, Vincent, would have joined him, but that particular day something came up and José decided to head out alone. He was in one of the vineyards much like Catala, working his way down and then back up again. It wasn't too hot, but it was getting late. He slipped, and his knee went straight into one of the wooden posts used to train younger vines. José went down like a sack. He was only 20 metres down the hill from the truck but he couldn't move. He reached for his phone. His pocket was empty. The phone was sat on the dashboard of the truck. The vineyard's miles away from anywhere. There was no one close by walking a dog or spraying their own vines. It was just José, lying alone on the side of the hill, immobile and with too much dead weight strapped to his back. Somehow he managed to twist his way off of the chemical tank and started making his way back up the slope. With all his mass on the loose topsoil, he started many an avalanche and for every inch or so up, he lost a half inch back down again. Two steps forward, one step back. There was no question of putting any weight at all on the leg. It was too excruciating. José is not of slight build.

It took two hours of slipping, sweating and swearing to crawl the 20 metres up the hill. Eventually, he managed to get back to the truck and pull himself up into the cab. He grabbed his phone. It had no signal. Fuck.

Eventually, Vincent came looking for him. He missed dinner. José would never miss dinner. The doctors told him later that it would have been harder to damage the knee more than he did. He tore his ACL (anterior cruciate ligament) and the rest: all the tendons and muscles around his knee were utterly shredded. The doctor gave strict instructions for José: he was to do absolutely nothing, put no weight on it, for months, perhaps even a year, during his recovery; certainly no picking of grapes or heavy lifting. Even driving the truck was off-limits. Of course, doctor's orders were not quite the irresistible object coming against the immovable force of Catalan machismo and the needs and requirements of harvest. Later that year, José was driving the truck and grabbing heavy things and wincing at the weight on his knee. He didn't pick, though, and by the end realised that heavy-lifting was definitely a no-no. His knee's still in dreadful shape, but he does everything he can, and several things he probably shouldn't, all year round.

Soon the rains let off and spring gives way to more summer-like weather. You may do some green harvesting if there looks to be quite a lot of grapes. Green harvesting occurs throughout the wine world. Mostly used during large vintages, it's a practice in which you cut off some of the bunches in order to promote concentration of flavour and vigour among the remaining grapes. This only works if you cut those bunches off before veraison – preferably some time before. There are certain grapes for which this is essential – our Mourvèdre, for instance, is always clipped down to three bunches per vine before harvest. If we don't do that, there isn't enough concentration in the juice to counter balance the tannins in the grapes' thick skins.

As well as green harvesting, it's the constant tending to the vines, keeping track of growth rates and dealing with any issues that may come up, be it rot, weeds or insects. The heat comes, as do the tourists. Folks begin flocking to the beach and even the standard lunch break might include a dip in the sea.

Bizarrely, the closer vintage gets, the further away it can begin to seem.

The pain finally ceased in my right hand. It only took about ten months. I did something to it last vintage, I'm not sure what it was precisely, but I think it came about trying to unscrew the nozzle of a hose as quickly as possible. It felt like a muscle tear, around the bones that eventually become the middle and index finger. I'm at the age now, and have the sort of ailments, that means something is always sore. I never knew the spectrum of sore before, however, and now I can differentiate between things that are just sore (my ankles, knees, neck and right shoulder are just sore, pretty much permanently, in various stages of intensity) and things that are hurt. My hand was hurt. I thought for a while that it might always be hurt (which would lead to it moving from being hurt to being sore). That as my early middle-age gave way to middle middle-age and then late middle-age, I might start referring to it as my 'bad hand'. It would have been well-situated, being on the same side as my 'bad shoulder'. All my other bad limbs are not limited by labels such as 'left' and 'right' and refuse to work in beautiful symmetry.

With that pain gone, so goes the last of the previous vintage's injuries. Some of scars remain, of course. But for the most part, I'll be whole when I go back. My hands have gone soft again, smooth to the touch, and bearing the minimal blemishes of someone who spends most days writing with a keyboard. Even the callous by the last joint of my right middle finger, the one that rises and hardens from the way I hold my pen, is merely a minor lump at the moment.

I've read that some martial artists punch iron to toughen their hands and prepare them for the rigours of combat. I wonder what manner of routine could be concocted for winemakers, to get their hands vintage-ready before vintage, or if it would even do any good. Vintage hands are both the blessing and curse of winemaking. The few days before the callouses form, the cuticles are shorn down to the quick, leaving nothing left to snag or tear, before the muscles in your hands remember what it's like to need their own power, not just the hands but the fingers, able to lift and to balance at any angle hanging from a ladder or balancing a comporte demands. It's not strength that comes from weights or can really be planned for. The fingers take the brunt, because so many things are right on the edge of going wrong. There are so many points where something is about to happen and someone screams 'wait!' and all the purchase you have left, the difference between disaster and salvation, is what strength and balance you have in the final knuckles of your middle three fingers.

I don't think punching iron would help.

It's why I always think of the whites as tougher than the reds, even though there's far more red, and so much more work. By the time the reds come, my muscles and hands are ready for it. The friction burns from shovelling the *marc* of the white stems speeds up the hardening of the palms and pads, as does the relentless speed of those changes and the violence of loading the press compared to the (relatively) gentle nature of loading the de-stemmer.

We don't use gloves for much in the winery because we build our own. And just to make sure the callouses take, we rinse our hands constantly. We need to. Grape juice is sticky. A spray with the hose, a dip in the ever-present water/SO2 mix, these things happen 20 or 30 times a day. They have to.

Then the reds come in and your hands aren't just battered and raw, they're stained. There is an old winery trick that keeps the tannins and dye from building up too quick. It's genius. Someone explained how it worked to me once, but I'd rather not be reminded. I like the magical logic of the solution. After processing reds, and sorting through the fruit, or hand-punching barrels and that sort thing, with your hands caked in pigment and tannin and the very essence of colour, march your way over to the waste section of the de-stemmer and rub the discarded stems over your hands thoroughly. The result is amazing. It doesn't get off the deep stuff, the bits that fill the gaps, but it gets enough that by the end of vintage you don't look like you have circulation problems. Unless, of course, by the end of vintage you really do have circulation problems. In which case, you should see someone.

So by the time the whites are processed and fermenting away, we have our gauntlets. We've built the shield around our hands. It's only leather armour, but it will do. It's, at times, excruciating to construct. It's not just the muscle and the callous that contributes, but the scar tissue as well. All the wounds gained in those first weeks, the cuts and the scrapes, they scar quickly and add to the armour. You'll be grateful for it later. And once the armour is built, you get the reds to give it colour.

I looked at my fingerprints, on both hands, and they weren't a pretty sight. The pigment of a million or more grape skins stained the grooves between the ridges. Cuts sliced perpendicular to their idiosyncratic patterns. Never parallel. My cuticles ragged and dyed. The nails unintentionally painted. My palms, pads and fingers felt of sandpaper.

I wrote that when I returned from my first harvest. I was working as a sommelier at the time, and my customers were somewhat concerned that, as far as appearances went, my hands didn't seem fit for service. My boss thought it was hilarious. A simple explanation to the diners as I poured was all that was required.

'Please pardon the appearance of my hands; I've just been making wine in the Roussillon,' I would say. And they seemed to be fine with that.

Soon, however, the stains and scars faded. I no longer needed to apologise for the appearance of my hands. Without constant battering, they regained their softness. Lifting the occasional case of wine seemed pedestrian. It took only three weeks for all the pigment to disappear. After two months, the scars had faded. And in ten weeks, the last rasping callous had returned to its soft and lazy state.

They're whole, healthy. Ready to do it all again.

ZZ TOP & ROLLERCOASTERS

O N A DUSTY, SUNNY DAY IN JULY, WE DROVE though some vineyards just outside (or in? it's so hard to tell with Argelès) Argelès. It was what summer days are supposed to be. Crystal clear but for perhaps a dissipating jet trail or two. The Med like topaz. A breeze blew, but there was no Tramontane gale. It was gentle and cooled off the spot where a bit of sweat collected at the back of my neck. You could hear the vines growing around us as we pulled up to the single house sat in the midst of all these ripening grapes. This is where Julien's dad lives, and he owns the vines that surrounded us. He built the house here himself. It's not quite high enough to see the sea, but it faces in that direction any-way. We had popped by to pick up a few tools and he cracked open a beer for us, asking us what we expected from the impending harvest. We chatted and then he said something to Andy and motioned towards me, laughing at the eternal joke of me coming here on my holidays. He then moved back to wine, and asked about the vines and how they're going. He's grown grapes for decades. He's a giant, bearded Catalan who used to be a baker and never misses an opportunity to speak whimsically of the misbehaviour of his youth. When he's with Julien, Julien takes on the look of someone very quickly embarrassed by their dad. I know the look well. I've perfected it. But at that moment it was just the man and us talking business and sipping beer – no tales of the whorehouses in Jonquera or whatever other border town he used to visit, just shop chat about when harvest will be and how big it looks. He knew most of it of course, most of the vines are his, or used to be. But he wanted to be kept in the loop; to keep his ear to the ground even as he enjoyed his semi-retirement.

Waiting for grapes to ripen is kind of like a roller coaster. The winter is waiting in the queue, worrying for a minute that you're not tall enough to get on in the first place (OK, like a roller coaster when you're a little kid) and that when you finally get to the very front of the line, the gate will close before you while you wait for yet another round until you can get on. Then, you get on, and you're excited, because this is very, very different from not being on a roller coaster. Bud break is kind of like when they bring down the safety bar in front of you. There's no going back once the safety bar comes down. There's also no going back once the buds break because time is linear and only moves in one direction. Spring is very much the inching forward at low altitude. Every loud 'ka-chung' of the winch is a shoot shooting or a leaf opening, or the very, very tiny pre-grapes forming. And all of those things bring you a little bit higher up. It takes a few months – it's a slow roller coaster – but my goodness does it go high up. There are undulations along the way. Heavy downpours, hailstorms and the ridiculous winds that ravage these slopes. Hopefully, if you're very lucky and have made ample sacrifices to both Dionysus and the weather gods, these will be slight undulations. The sort of undulations that would suit a roller coaster for your bratty kid brother who's too scared of heights to really tackle the big ones. If it's a bad growing season, those undulations are crazier than the final slam; the loop where you actually go all the way upside down and around. And then there's that final slam. That crazy peak that the roller coaster has been inching its way up to all this time? That peak is called veraison. Veraison is when the berries finish their growth and start to ripen. It's sort of like grape puberty. It's at this point, if the weather is willing, that the roller coaster begins its plunge towards vintage. If the grapes are red grapes, this is when they begin to develop their colour, changing from the green that all grapes start with. At this point, in this part of the world, and barring hail or some other catastrophe, you really have an idea of how big your harvest is going to be. This is good, because this is when you do the final bits of hiring and preparation for the harvest. If you know it's going to be a big one, you might look for a few more pickers. If veraison comes early, and the weather looks good, you might ask those pickers to come a week or so earlier than you normally would have. You want warmth and you want sunlight.

One year, in July, veraison set in quite early, and folks were predicting both a bumper harvest and a high quality one that was going to start very, very early. And so everyone readied themselves for such an event. The weather was hot and, strangely for this dry corner of France, quite humid. Veraison set in just about festival season, when the party-loving folks at Château Valmy hold their big 'Les Déferlantes' festival. Château Valmy is one of the few wine estates in the region that would look right on a post card. A big, Victorian era château with a similarly large winery surrounded by impeccably manicured vines. They even put flower baskets on the end of their vine rows. To be fair, there is some evidence that this provides some manner of distraction for hungry aphids that might otherwise feast on the vines, but I reckon they're intention is purely decorative. Of course, the wine isn't all that great, but at least the place is pretty to look at and they've spent bajillions on it, which is good for the region and all that. Personally, I think it would be better for the region if they put all that effort into making amazing wine, but I think that might be a little old fashioned on my part.

However, they do hold a fucking cool music festival every year. That particular year saw both ZZ Top and Arcade Fire headlining. I went the night of Arcade Fire, which was awesome, but I'd be lying if I said I didn't want to see ZZ Top that little bit more. The nice thing about this festival is that it's not an overnight camping thing. It doesn't have to be. The camping population of Argelès over the summer is ridiculous; it's like 70,000 people or some small city's population like that. So once the gigs are over for the night, everyone gets on the 'Petit Train' (The Petit Train is not a train. It's a jeep that's made up to look like a train, and has several 'carriages' that it tows along. Both Argelès and Collioure have a few of these that run for the tourists, taking them around and showing them the sights. The stop for it in Collioure is right by the Sola, and often we'll sit sipping a beer whilst watching the tourists pile into the train, cameras dangling around their necks.), which takes them back to town and swings by all the campsites, and you don't have to stand knee-deep in mud. Which is just as well, as the night of the Arcade Fire gig, a storm rocked in off the Mediterranean that behaved as though it had got lost on its way from the Caribbean during hurricane season. You could see it, flashes of lightning in the distance followed by the inevitable echoes of thunder. It started off so far away. Like a storm in a story. But it just kept getting closer, and the thunder got louder, like approaching footsteps. And then something happened that I'd only seen in the movies. There was a bolt of lightning, so bright it was as though a giant paparazzi had taken a group photo of the entire festival-going crowd, thunder like a bomb, and following the thunder, a downpour that fell so hard the drops hurt. Almost instantly, everything was wet. It was like a monsoon. We ran down to the Petit Train, as did most of the other folks. Poor Arcade Fire had to finish the set early for fear of electrocution. They seemed like very nice folks. I think maybe they're Canadians.

It could have been a disaster, but it wasn't. There were more than enough trains for everyone and no one panicked. People were wet and had to go home early, but no one was an asshole about it. We dried out and had a dram and it was fine.

But that storm marked the beginning of some weird weather for the post-veraison season. Afterwards it was hot and sunny but hazy, in a way not seen very often in those parts and, unbeknownst to us, it was doing some funny things to the grapes. Without the right amounts of direct sunlight, the bunches were ripening very, very unevenly. Even the random sampling wasn't showing the extent of this at the time; it was only when harvest came that we realised the bunches had variances of up to five degrees – some grapes at 14% potential alcohol and some at only 9%. It was crazy. It threw the entirety of harvest out of whack, adding an extra three or four weeks to it and nearly breaking many of us involved (I was close to emotionally dead by about three weeks in – it was a huge harvest and seemed never ending). That was a big and unexpected undulation on the roller coaster of ripening. And we didn't even really notice it as it was happening.

Summer isn't just a time of ripening. It's a time of partying. Andy and Kirsten got married in the summer down here and prepared for it in the single greatest way ever. They made a fortified wine for their wedding. They picked some old vine

Grenache Noir in 2007 that weighed in at 18.5% potential alcohol, basket pressed it themselves, fortified it to 17% and put it in a 100 litre tank for people to help themselves to at the nuptials. Of course, that wasn't the only wine at the wedding. There were bottles and magnums of Coume del Mas and Mas Cristine everywhere, as well as 16 magnums of Champagne to kick things off. But having a vat of fortified wine available on tap, well, I don't think many folks attending, even the locals, had seen that before. The wedding took place up in the hills above town, just down from the Catala vineyard and just above the Consolation vineyard, at an old hermitage (the one that gave the Consolation vines their name). The Petit Train brought us all up. It was a small affair, attended by good friends and family from all over the world. We ate outside, on long picnic tables, with beautiful bouillabaisse, BBQ meat, salad, cheese and charcuterie. The wedding cake was made by local chocolatier genius Olivier Baijard, who sculpted a crown for for it adorned with a chocolate wine bottle, grapes and an artist's palette and brush. We feasted and danced. The band included the best man, Tim, and Andy himself, with Kirsten on the tambourine with her mate, Hannah, with Broomie on bongos, guitar and vocals and Sheep on guitar and vocals. I got up to sing at one point, confidence boosted by the 'Vin d'Marriage'. No one threw anything at me or disconnected the mic, so I assume my performance wasn't too disastrous.

Andy was the first to grab an empty carafe and fill it up. I think people were a little scared to begin with. I followed suit. Soon, everyone was filling them up, and as the meal wore on, the advice to add a bit of water, a perfectly reasonable continental thing to do, was lost utterly. There was no Petit Train to pick us up, even though one had taken us there. Instead we followed, very drunkenly, a path carved through the vines. I found myself nearly falling down many of the same vines that I would nearly fall down a few months later during my first attempt at picking. That walk back took us under the span of the large Viaduct du Douy, the bridge that brings the motorway over the valley and through the mountain; a fast route to Port-Vendres. It was supposed to go on to Banyuls, but construction stopped when the money ran out. So this fast bit of road runs right up until the outline of what should have been another tunnel, and instead breaks into a rounda-bout that brings you to various exits into the town and another hairpin, sheer-drop, too-narrow for proper traffic really, road that, because it is treacherous and in France, attracts too many cyclists for there to be any comfort whatsoever. I find those roads dangerous enough as it is, without worrying about whether there's a lycra-clad lunatic about to sneak between me and the short concrete wall that separates me from a long drop through steep cliffs and vines.

Of course, that evening, wandering through down the path through cascading vine leaves with the heavy swagger that fortified wine brings, there was no thought of driving. And the cars on the bridge above couldn't see the kilt-clad reveller descending below them. At the base of the valley the town meets the vines and overlaps somewhat, with rows in place of what may have been someone's backyard. Emerging from the vines in kilts earned more than a glance or two from the kids playing football in the street. Drunkenly muttered 'bonjours' and the odd attempts at thumbs up and grins brought their incredulous stares quickly to giggles. It was all good. There seemed a bubble of good will surrounding us. We looked ridiculous to them, and were obviously drunk, but there was no shouting or bad behaviour. Just the sheen of a good time that was to continue, apparently, at the Piano Bar, then still in the capable hands of Michel. And still with a remarkable selection of Trappist beers.

Because after an entire day drinking Banyuls, an extraordinarily strong beer brewed by monks in Belgium makes the perfect nightcap. I had to be carried home that night. The next day the sun burned off the hangover of the night before and it was as though the wedding never ended. Everyone just changed into more comfy clothes and kept going. We barbecued in the back garden behind the Sola and drank cold beer slowly. Nobody took their sunglasses off.

Weddings, festivals, parties of all shapes and sizes; there's a great deal of enjoyment had in the summer here.

In early September the artists of Collioure celebrate their own harvest festival. They lay down proper turf along the Rue de la Fraternité for *'le déjeuner sur l'herbe'*. It's mostly an 'end of season' festival, heralding the end of the summer and celebrating a, hopefully, successful three or four months selling sculptures and canvases, prints and posters. The ateliers and galleries will often pour wine and friends, acquaintances and passers-by will wander along the freshly-turfed lane, marvelling at a street covered in grass, window shopping or actually shopping. They often get bands for the evenings and the music sometimes goes on long past what would be considered reasonable for a quiet seaside town.

It's another sign of the shifting calendar; the impending rustle of dry leaves and emptying of the region as people leave their holidays and return to whatever form of reality from whence they came.

It was the beginning of August, and we sat outside as the sun set over Loch Indaal. The water turned a deep sapphire while the whitewash along the side of the Bowmore distillery glowed in the waning light. A breeze kicked in from the water, raising a bit of chop on that deep sapphire and bringing a bite to the air. The girls' hair whipped in the wind while I poured the wine for everyone. We started with Folio, the Collioure Blanc from Coume del Mas, and I spoke a few words about the wine. It was a bottle from my first vintage there; they all were. The folks at the table heckled a bit, but without malice. We were all friends.

I talked about the wine and the place it came from. Most of the people there knew Andy as well, and some had tried the wines. We'd fired up the barbecue and the wine flowed. It wasn't a formal tasting – they'd just asked me to say a few words. It felt odd, stood in the garden of a cottage on a loch, next to a distillery, to be talking about wine and France.

When I've these wines around me, the Roussillon is never far. I open a bottle of wine that I've helped make and I go back there in my mind. It's like a reflex. And so sitting with friends on a patio on Islay, off the west coast of Scotland, I was back in the sun of the Roussillon, lifting comportes off the back of Julien's truck to empty into the de-stemmer, smelling the ferments and the sweet honeysuckle of the Grenache.

I set the empties up on the sea wall and positioned my camera to take in the bottles and the distillery in the background. It was before twilight, but after sunset; the sky's darkening pastel shades framed in contrast the sea and shadowed hills in the distance. I wanted a record of these two places together, the juice of the grape next to where the juice of the grain came from. It was a strange sensation, to be so perfectly happy and content where I was, in such a beautiful corner of the world, and still to feel an impatience to be elsewhere, and to get started again.

DRY BOOTS & DIRTY T-SHIRTS

M Y SUMMERS ARE SPENT IN ANTICIPATION.
The other day, I read about a hailstorm that
destroyed the crop in Vouvray, to the north in the
Loire Valley. A region famous for its remarkable white wines
made from the Chenin Blanc grape, in all manner of method
– still, sparkling, sweet, medium and bone dry though all of
them with the texture of beeswax. I love the wines from
there; sort of like Collioure, they're an oft-overlooked gem
and reminder of just how diverse France can be when it
comes to winemaking. And because of a freak storm, for at
least a year, there will be little to no new wine. Something
similar happened in Provence two years before. I wonder
when it's our turn.

I remember driving through Burgundy one June, seeing
towering thunderheads spread along the length of the Côte
d'Or, bolts of lightning forking down, reaching towards the
vineyards below. For most it would seem like just another
summer storm. I mentioned to the friend I was driving with, a
nice chap named Ben, another Luvians veteran, that the
storm would likely wind up in vintage reports. That much wet
so early in the growing season means more treatment and
triage in the vines, more work for what usually winds up being
less wine.

Reports this year from all of France's major wine growing regions are gloomy. Winter lasted longer than expected, and spring never really had its bright ending. Vineyards in Burgundy are covered in flood water, and the Bordelais are trying to put a positive spin on it, saying that the impending late harvest for this season will bring a more 'classical' style of wine. But everyone's nervous. At the end of the day, it's farming; we make an agricultural product, and a bad vintage makes an already difficult job that much worse, with a lot less gained from it. Consumers don't tend to taste it as much. Good winemakers can succeed in all but the most difficult circumstances. The bottles don't look any different if the wine was harder to make from one year to the next. Often there will be less of it, so there's less revenue for much more effort. At least when it arrives, when the grapes start coming in and the press is ready to go, there's too much to do to wallow in anguish and whinge about how shitty everything is.

I check my weather app at least once a day. Andy emails me. It's not hot yet down there. There's no endless sunshine yet. The hallmarks of summer in Banyuls and Collioure are sadly lacking so far. It's not about how hot it gets, it's more about the sunshine. You want there to be a lot of sun from the end of April until the solstice (and even more after the solstice). As soon as the days start getting shorter, it gets more and more important for the leaves to get as much unbroken light as possible to feed the fruit. Usually, in this part of the world, this is something we don't worry too much about. The sun comes out in the Roussillon, it always does. It's why the tourists flock here in their droves, and why grapes have been grown here for millennia. But instead the rains have lasted longer than normal, and the sun often loses the fight with the cloud. Some producers, in some wine-producing regions, are wealthy enough to send aircraft into storm clouds, releasing vapours in hopes of breaking up hail stones; dissolving them into rain. We are not really in the league yet of trying to control the weather, nor do I think we ever will be.

Andy jokes that when there is too much rain, when the sun doesn't come out for long enough, it results in an AC/DC vintage – there's A Whole Lotta Rosé. The reds won't gain enough ripeness or complexity to make compelling wines, and so many of them will be pressed instead for rosé. Julien and José will be working relentlessly from now until harvest to make sure that the grapes get as much sun as possible. They'll thin the canopy of leaves, which we normally leave untouched in order to protect the grapes, in order to get more exposure. With all the rain, they'll wander the vines to make sure rot doesn't set in. For them it's months of nurture in the lead up to a harvest that looks to be the latest in decades.

But we don't know for sure. Vines, in spite of their care, treatment and nurturing, sometimes perform to their own accord. The rest of the summer could have record sunshine going straight through until October. It could still be the best vintage ever; the vintage of the century. We do everything in our power until we're powerless. In the meantime, until we know for sure, there's still quite a bit to be done.

Just before vintage, at Mas Cristine, we'll run the bottling line one more time for the previous year's red. We need the tanks free for the new harvest. It's a hearty appetiser for the brutal work to come, and it's good to crack open a newly minted bottle of last year's wine before making this year's wine.

As well as bottling, there's also one last special bit of racking. Hidden in a corner of Mas Cristine, there's a small tank. It holds only three hectolitres, and during vintage comes in handy for storing press juice from small vineyards before it's blended with something else. It will be used several times over the course of harvest. But when vintage ends, it serves a different purpose.

We make two fortified sweet wines at Mas Cristine: a Muscat de Rivesaltes and a Rivesaltes Ambré. The former is a light, fresh, slightly flinty style of wine. It's bottled less than a year after harvest and will be aged only in tank. We keep it as fresh as possible, and do everything in our power not to let air get to it. The latter is aged in barrels, from a small amount of the Muscat saved at the end of each harvest. It would be a solera, but we keep it upstairs, on the landing above our little winemaking area at the cave co-op. It's a very oxidative style of wine, and the vintages are blended together as and when we add to the barrels. The quantities are so small, and the logistics of topping up the barrels upstairs with the latest wine so delicate, that we can't use a pump.

So in the last days or weeks before harvest, we go about as old school as it gets in terms of winemaking. I grab a bucket and open the tank of leftover Muscat (which may have some sweet Macabeu or Grenache Gris added to it as well), and dip it in, filling it just over halfway, and carry it up the stairs to the Ambré solera. Using a funnel, I pour carefully and top up the barrels, making sure not to overfill or spill. That's why I only put a little bit more than half a bucket in in the first place. This is another good primer for things to come: you mustn't spill anything, and there's nothing about it you can rush, or do half-assed, because if you do? You'll probably spill something.

Rivesaltes Ambré is what Mas Cristine was famous for in the past. When Philippe and Julien took over the domaine, there was no stock in the deal, and so they had to start from scratch. It's taken six years for our solera to build up enough to bottle a batch. It's never going to be a wine that we make vast quantities of (before they took it over, it was the only wine Mas Cristine produced), but it's a traditional wine that we're all proud to continue to make. The size of the solera is such that we'll only be able to bottle a batch every three years or so, but as it gets older, as the oldest wines in the bottoms of those barrels gain more and more complexity, every bottling will hopefully improve.

The tank evacuated of Muscat after a long afternoon of lugging buckets; it's cleaned and put back into its place. All the tanks are empty now along the alley in Mas Cristine. Empty and waiting.

I own a lot of t-shirts. They sit, folded with reasonable competence, in three piles, on the top shelf of my closet. Two of the piles are the t-shirts I wear regularly, pretty much everyday. Those are the two front piles and they're stacked high. The shirts in those piles are varied – some are beer freebies, many are Red Sox tees, and quite a few possess quirky graphics or phrases that appeal to whatever mood I was in when I bought them. I like my t-shirts to have some sort of meaning to me. I don't know why.

The third pile is smaller and sits in their shadow, tucked in at the back. I have to take out one of the other piles to get to them. Those shirts are not worn everyday, or even monthly. They get worn pretty much once a year.

Technically speaking, they're clean. They've been thoroughly laundered and detergent, be it Ecover, Bold or Persil, has done all it can for them. They don't look clean. The white ones, if they can still be called that, bear the full brunt; splattered and smeared with uneven blotches of grey, black and jaundiced brown, front and back, sleeve and chest and belly, looking for all the world as though I'd slaughtered something long ago whilst wearing them.

It's the mark of grapes in their thousands and perhaps millions.

Out came that third pile this morning. I lay them on my bed, smiled, refolded each one and packed them tightly into my duffel bag. Each one has several vintages worth of wine-making stains so deeply pummelled into the fabric that they must be now a part of it. Tomorrow I'll start pummelling the sixth vintage into them, and I couldn't be happier about it.

And then I'm back. My place isn't ready yet, so I crash with Andy and Kirsten for the first few days. I'm used to their pull-out couch, and Theo and Angus are great kids. Andy and I will blind-test each other on wines before dinner and Kirsten will either roll her eyes or chuckle at our nerdy chat. Theo calls me 'Big Rich' and is fond of playing air guitar to AC/DC. Angus eats as though at the age of two he's determined to play forward for Scotland next year. Theo looks like his dad and Angus looks like his mum. That's what I see, at least. Some nights we'll go downstairs to the gallery with a bottle of malt and the three of us will drink and chat into the night. Sometimes, if things aren't too busy yet. Andy will smoke cigarettes and select a decent playlist on iTunes.

I like these brief stays with the family at vintage. It pushes back some of the loneliness that the work can bring.

It's dark when I hear the shower go. I'm awake, but the difference between consciousness and unconsciousness is minimal. Sleep is plagued by work-dreams. Tanks that need filled, leaks discovered, winemaking in the slow-motion miasma and unreality of the dreamworld. Often I wake in a panic, needing to focus on the objects around me and remind myself that they are not hoses, pumps, barrels and grape bins, but a cupboard, a television, a pile of toys, a dining room table. Sometimes it's humid and the pull out bed is damp with my sweat. I lie there in the darkness, listening to the shower upstairs, holding these few moments close to myself, knowing that this will be my last bit of rest for 13 or 14 hours. Knowing that it wasn't enough. I slowly open and close my hands, trying to work the arthritic rust from my knuckles. They're swollen and sore. I hear Andy walking down the stairs and sit up in bed. He's never had to wake me. I'm ready and get out of bed as he walks in and switches on the kitchen light. He flicks the kettle on and checks emails while I get myself ready. We have a cuppa. If there's no time for cereal, we'll pick up a couple of pain au chocolat on the walk to the car. I check the Red Sox score. They've not been very good for the last few vintages. We'll chat a bit about the plans for the day. What grapes are coming from where. I rub my eyes and massage my temples and still try to get my hands working. Sometimes I'll take my cup to the small balcony in the kitchen. The street is a small canyon in the old town of Collioure. The buildings are terraced, tall and narrow. The street-lights are sepia toned and the street is barely wide enough for a car. They rarely drive down here anyway. Usually it's just the bin men, clearing the rubbish in the wee hours, before the tourists can see it. There always seems to be an echo on this street, even when it's quiet. The road itself is cobbled brick, angled downward towards a central gutter. It's dry here, but when it rains, it runs off the dry soil in the hills, through the town and towards the sea. The streets become mountain streams and the rainwater comes down in torrents.

But hopefully not at harvest. Not when I'm stood on the balcony in the morning, sipping tea and passing my sleepy eyes over the yellow halos that surround the street lights, or up into the sky to see it pass from black to dark blue.

We leave quietly. If I'm lucky, my boots are dry.

We walk upwards towards the centre of town and I look back and I see Theo, Andy's oldest, stood on the balcony. He holds the rail with one hand and a blue beach pale in the other and looks at us through the bars. His eyes are wide and eyebrows raised in a mixture of hope and longing. I think he wants his dad to turn around, to tell him to come along and join us. Andy doesn't turn around, and I don't tell him what I see. I look back once more and he hasn't moved, hasn't said a word. His eyes glimmer in the pale light and I know he'll stay there until we round the corner out of view. He'll go back to sleep and have a full day. He'll drive his mother crazy and most likely treat his little brother Angus as older brothers do. But for a few moments in the morning, he wanted more than anything to go to work with his dad. And for a second I remember being in Boston, three or four years old, watching my dad walk out the door in his suit, holding a briefcase, wanting to do the exact same thing.

POSTSCRIPT &
ACKNOWLEDGEMENTS

I JUST RECEIVED WORD THAT THE WEATHER'S turned in Collioure and the sun has arrived at last. Too much of it, of course, and so there's considerable stress on the vines, they've been chucked from the fridge into the sauna. I've no idea what will happen come harvest.

Every time I board the flight back to Britain at the end of harvest, I wonder why I'm leaving. This small corner of France that I've described here has become very much like a home to me. It's odd that these aches and pains and the constant grind are followed by a deep sense of loss at their completion. Be that as it may, it is not an easy place to leave, and I am thankful that the cycle of viticulture (and the patience of Andy, Philippe and Julien) keeps me coming back.

At the back of this book, you will find a long list of names of the people who made it happen, by pledging their support long before I had finished writing it, most with absolutely no idea what a book by me would look like. Some are old friends, and some strangers. But all of them made this happen, and I couldn't be happier or more thankful that their names are listed there for posterity.

However, there are people whose contributions to this book require separate mention and particular thanks. Without whom, there would have been no book to support.

Andy Cook got me into this. He taught me my first lessons in wine, and I don't think I've learned more in my life from anyone else that isn't my parents. Whether it's exchanging emails over the delicate subject of minerality in wine, listening to AC/DC at full volume whilst drinking tequila or staying up until dawn drinking whisky and discussing the universe, I cannot thank him enough for guidance he's given and the confidence he's shown in me.

While Andy's been brilliant, special mention must also go to his wife, Kirsten. I arrive as the harbinger of the year's most difficult time, and yet she still manages to be happy to see me and make me feel incredibly welcome. She's one of the strongest people I know, a brilliant mother bringing up two great kids, and a ridiculously talented artist. I'm pretty sure she can drink more Banyuls than me as well.

Philippe Gard and Julien Grill of Coume del Mas and Mas Cristine keep letting me come back every year. These are not hobby wineries, nor are they vanity projects for retired bankers. These are two of the best wineries in the whole of the south of France, and to be brought back year-after-year is a tremendous compliment. Their friendliness and patience with my terrible French, even in times of urgency, has been amazing. For the incredible cheeses and the certainty that there will be cold beer in the fridge, they have my immense gratitude. It's been an honour to be a part of their team for all these years, and I'm looking forward to doing it again. To José and Vincent, and their *vendangeurs*, and to Justin, Kiwi Johnny, Elysia, Olivier, Adele, Thibault and all the other *stagaires* over the years, who've taught me that there

[176]

aren't any tricks and that none of the short-cuts are worth it, cheers and beers at the end of the day.

While Andy got me into wine, it was Xander Cansell that got me into Unbound. Xander has been there pretty much every step of the way, and a fair few before the journey started. His support and general optimism that everything will get sorted somehow, usually by him sorting it, has made what could have been daunting quite the opposite. It's quite a remarkable company, this shiny new publisher, and it's exciting to be a part of it. I couldn't imagine doing this with anyone else.

Others from Unbound that should get mention are Rachael Kerr, John Mitchinson, Dan Kieran, Isobel Frankish, Caitlin Harvey, Cathy Hurren and Justin Pollard. Rachael edited the manuscript and ensured that I wasn't terrified of getting feedback. John, Dan and Justin had belief and enthusiasm for both the project and my ability, which gave me confidence when it was running low. Caitlin and Isobel have been there right from the very beginning, and manage to work so bloody hard with so much on their plates whilst still managing to smile that I think they'd be rather good at working harvest someday.

For their patience and understanding, I owe Robin, James, Damon, Lucia, Roz and Tammy at Swig Wines a great deal of thanks and probably a few hours overtime. It's not easy writing a book and working a day job, but nor is it easy working with someone writing a book and working a day job.

Much of this book was written and laid out in my local pub, The Black Lion. It's a great pub. The owner, Peter, and the manager, Buzz, and their staff have been absolutely brilliant in raising awareness for the book. I moved back to London when I started writing this book, and felt a bit out of place.

The folks at the Lion made me feel at home again, and couldn't have been more supportive. It's amazing how many of both the staff and the regulars there can find their names in the back of this book.

To Frances: whenever I taste something brilliant and singular, whenever I see a sausage dog, whenever I see art where I didn't expect to, I think of her and wonder what she'd make of it all. And now I'm curious, and slightly nervous, wondering what she'll make of this book.

I can't write anything to do with wine without crediting J. Gilmour Manuel, and his late wife Gilli. It was through them both that I was introduced to the tradition and ceremony of a traditional meal with its traditional vinous accompaniments. Gilmour taught me how to decant, using to test, with patience, many of the extraordinary and perfectly aged clarets and Burgundies from his cellar. It was him that first poured me a glass of Manzanilla before a meal, and it was Gilli that taught me what should go with it, and how to make it better. I wouldn't have been curious enough to seek my first job in wine without them. My gratitude to both of them extends far outside the confines of this book.

My career in the wine trade started at a small shop in Scotland owned by an Italian family. It was an incredible introduction to this remarkable world. And so to Vince and Tony, and to all the Fusaros and everyone I ever had the great fortune to work with at Luvians over the years, thank you.

And finally, to my parents, John and Elizabeth Bray, to whom this book is dedicated. Even though they doubt it sometimes, I'm pretty sure they brought me up right. And for that, I can never thank them enough.

WORDS & MEANINGS

Anthocyanins Pigment molecules that provide a great deal of the colour in grapes, particularly red ones.

Bon-bons Tremendous bottles that are quite round, and as such look like candies. Quite a lot of people age their Rancio Banyuls in these, and then leave them out in the direct sunlight to cook the wine.

Bordelais People from Bordeaux, generally, though usually referring to someone involved in wine in Bordeaux.

Bouchon A cork, but also the bung for the top hole of a barrel.

Cap The giant clump of skins and stems that floats on a cushion of CO_2 above the fermenting juice.

Casot A small hut or shed in the vines used for storing water and tools and the like. Ridiculously quaint-looking, even when dilapidated.

Catalan Someone from Catalonia. Also the language of Catalonia.

Catalonia A culturally distinct region that stretches from north-east Spain to south-west France along the Mediterranean side, pretty much from Barcelona to Perpignan. Collioure and Banyuls are in French-Catalonia.

Cathars Also known as Albigensians. Thirteenth-century heretics who were the targeted both by the papacy and French crown. They were eliminated in a brutal crusade and built remarkable castles.

Distingués Big beers in the Roussillon. But still less than a pint.

Élevage This is the ageing and raising of wine after fermentation but before bottling. In some cases it is just a case of leaving it in a tank for a few months, but more often there's blending, racking and stirring of the lees to take care of as well.

Ferment or **Fermentation** The conversion of sugar into alcohol by yeast. The yeast may be indigenous or 'natural', living on the grape skins in the vines, or it could come freeze-dried in a bag, kind of like the yeast you use to make bread at home. The latter needs to be added to the grape juice to start the process (called inoculation), while the former is already there, and will start the process whether you're ready for it or not. Usually not.

Fine Lees The fine lees are mostly dead yeast cells that, after feasting mightily on the grape sugars and frantically converting them into alcohol, fall quietly to the bottom of the fermentation vessel, be it barrel or tank. There may be some smaller particulate matter mixed in as well. The fine lees can influence the flavour of the wine considerably (if allowed to – you can always rack the wine off these to reduce influence) – they provide texture and can deepen flavours. Some folks encourage this by stirring them frequently during élevage. We don't tend to stir that much.

Fortification Adding nearly pure alcohol to wine during fermentation to preserve sweetness.

Frogbus The remarkably useful bus service that ferries folks from Girona to Perpignan.

Gross Lees The first batch of lees that settle at the bottom of the tank after wine has been pressed. These will be solids and particulate matter from the vines, including dead wasps, twigs, dirt, earwigs and the like. The 'gross' refers to the size of the bits, although they are pretty minging as well. We always rack the juice off the gross lees.

Lees General term for the detritus that settles at the bottom of the tank.

Phenols The stuff in wine that isn't fruity.

Pied de Cuve A small tank that is set aside to start the ferment; that is then subsequently added to larger tanks to start their ferment. Either it will have started its ferment naturally or have been inoculated. Larger volume tanks can sometimes take absolutely ages to start their fermentation, and so some of the juice may be bled off into a smaller vessel where it is easier to get things going. That juice, once it's begun its ferment, will then be added back into the larger tank.

Pigeage 'Punching down' in English. Where we grab a giant fork and push the cap into the fermenting juice that it's sitting on top of.

Press What we squish grapes in.

Racking Moving juice from one tank to the other. Sueterage in French. Usually to move juice off its lees.

Red Socks A Carignan Noir that I blend at Mas Cristine. Named after a baseball team but misspelled for legal reasons.

Red Sox A baseball team from Boston. Formerly the Boston 'Americans'. Responsible for insomnia and mood swings ranging from frustration and rage to euphoria, delight and childlike glee.

Remontage 'Pumping over' in English. This is when we pump the fermenting juice from the bottom of the tank over the skins at the top of the tank (called the cap).

Schist The prevailing soil-type in Collioure and Banyuls. Ancient clay that has turned to stone. Good for growing Grenache in all its rainbow of colours.

Stagaire Kind of an intern, but a winemaking intern. And they get paid.

Staves The long, curved planks that make up a barrel.

Vendangeur Picks grapes. Often hippies or hipsters.

Veraison The point at which the grapes stop growing and begin to ripen.

Vigneron A winemaker or proprietor/owner of a winery.

ZZ Top Texan Rock 'n' Blues band formed in 1969, noted for their massive beards.

VINES & BERRIES

THE GRAPES WE HARVEST. AS I MENTIONED before, this book is not meant to be a reference guide. However, we grow some grape varieties that fall somewhat outside the norm, and some that you might not be familiar with. So here they are; these are the grapes that we make wine from.

Carignan Gris This is quite a rare grape, even down here in its home territory. Pink/grey skin, with larger bunches than Grenache Gris, but with smaller berries. It's a late-ripener, and often we don't pick it until well after the rest of the whites are done, and the reds are midway through. Even then, it never gets fully ripe. Philippe has been known to mutter, whilst checking juice on the refractometer or chewing on a grape and spitting out the pips, that we could wait until Christmas and it still wouldn't get ripe. Instead of despairing about this, we use it to our advantage. We blend some in with the Mas Cristine Blanc and also produce a wine that is 100% Carignan Gris, called 'Petit Gris'. This is a racier, zingier white that what you normally find from the Roussillon. We like to think it has almost a Chablis-style.

Carignan Noir The oldest vines at Coume del Mas are Carignan vines. This is a rustic grape that manages to be both backwards and tannic, and flowery and fruity all at once. We tend to blend it with other grapes as it can be a little wild on its own, but of late we've started releasing one that I blended myself. It's called Red Socks and it's amazing.

Grenache Blanc A mutation of Grenache Noir that is, as its name suggests, white. We don't grow much Grenache Blanc. We prefer its peculiar cousin, Grenache Gris.

Grenache Gris 'Gris' means grey, and the grapes certainly sit somewhere between the dark blue/purple of red wine grapes and the bright green/yellow of white wine grapes. In some light they look grey, in some light they look pink. We love Grenache Gris. When picked from old vines and treated with the right care and attention it makes whites of good power and structure, with complex tropical fruit flavours. We also make a pale rosé from it, called 'Gris de Gris', which gets its pale colour from prolonged skin maceration.

Grenache Noir This is the bread and butter grape of the Roussillon. It thrives in the hot, dry summers and its bush vines are well-suited to withstand the battering of the Tramontane wind that comes from the mountains. Their skins are thin and they reach very high potential alcohol, which make them perfect for a region that make sweet, fortified wines. I always find a pale, honeysuckle white-fruit sweetness when I eat Grenache grapes, and that same sweetness comes through at the core of many Banyuls.

Macabeu This is called either Macabeo or Viura in Spain, and is famous as the main grape in both white Rioja and Cava. It grows in big bunches and can reach quite high potential alcohol. Quite a few places around here will use it instead of Muscat in Muscat de Rivesaltes as it's a bit less grumpy on the vine than Muscat. It's quite aromatic in style, but can also show full-bodied richness if yields are kept low and care is taken in selection.

Marsanne Cousin of Roussanne. More robust and perhaps slightly less perfumed. This goes into Mas Cristine Blanc and now we have 'Miranda' which is only Marsanne and also rather delicious.

Mourvèdre Tiny, dark berries that grow on big bunches, Mourvèdre is famous for its tannic grip. The local nickname for it is Etrangler chien, or 'The Dog Strangler' (we make a wine called The Dog Strangler as well). Biting into a ripe one is like biting into one of those Lindt chocolate balls. The skins are firm, hard and thick, giving the sense of crunching into a shell. The flesh and juice inside are sweet and somewhat blueberry like, but as you chew, you find yourself with a great deal more skin than flesh. This makes it a tricky customer, as you don't want a wine so tannic as to be undrinkable. We thin it out on the vine quite strictly, leaving only three bunches to harvest, in hopes of concentrating the juiciness of the berries and getting more balance between the juice and the skin.

Muscat There are a few different sorts of Muscat grapes kicking around these parts – there's the petit grain, which is used to make Muscat Sec, or dry Muscat – a light, aromatic style of wine that forms a perfect aperitif. And then there's gros grain (also called Muscat d'Alexandrie), which is sweet and smoky. Both are used to make our Muscat de Rivesaltes, the fortified sweet wine that used to be the bread and butter of this region. Muscat is remarkable in that it tastes of grapes. Wine grapes never taste of grapes, unless they're Muscat. Muscat also gets sold as an eating grape, sometimes for more money per kilo than a winery will pay for it. So growers will sell the Muscat for food and use bulk Macabeu to make their wine. This is considered quite naughty but often met with an unconcerned Gallic shrug when spoken about among winemakers and growers. Our Muscat de Rivesaltes just has Muscat in it, by the way.

Roussanne We can't get enough of Roussanne. Literally. It's scarce and delicious. Waxy and honeyed, it's one of the first varieties to achieve full ripeness in this neck of the woods. All that we have for Coume del Mas goes into C'est Pas d'Pipeau and the best at Mas Cristine gets split between Mas Cristine Blanc and 'Juliette', which is composed entirely of Roussanne and tastes rather delicious. While it's fermenting, it can often taste a little bit of iced tea.

Syrah A relatively recent addition to this part of the Roussillon, Syrah was brought here from the Rhône in the hopes that it would take to the terraces in the same way it does further North, producing deep, peppery reds.

It's not quite worked like that. Syrah vines in these parts need quite a bit of care and attention – the vines are not as robust as the bush vine Grenache, and has to be trellised on wires. This leaves them exposed in the harsh winds and often they suffer more than most in the occasional hailstorms that can hit in the late winter/early spring. However, when the fruit is good and ripe, the dark black berries look, even to the most novice eye, like something wonderful will come from them. Their stems seem luminous green on purple that looks as though carved from marble. And they taste good, too. And make brilliant, brilliant wine. Their juice is inky, and kind of ominous looking.

Vermentino We don't grow much of this grape, and what we do gets blended with Roussanne to make C'est Pas d'Pipeau. I always find it has kind of a salted porridge quality to it, in a really nice way. It's sometimes called Roll or Rolle elsewhere in France.

SUBSCRIBERS

UNBOUND IS A NEW KIND OF PUBLISHING house. Our books are funded directly by readers. This was a very popular idea during the late 18th and early 19th centuries. Now we have revived it for the internet age. It allows authors to write the books they really want to write and readers to support the writing they would most like to see published.

The names listed below are of readers who have pledged their support and made this book happen. If you'd like to join them, visit: www.unbound.co.uk.

Jonnie Adamson	Martin Baker	Emma Bentley
Bette Allen	Paul Baldwin	Frances Bentley
Fraser Anderson	Julian Barker	Terry Bergin
Andy Annett	Cameron J Barlow	David C. Bilas
Annie & Leon	Dr Helen Barratt	Stuart Birrell
Paul Arman	Michael Bartlett	Gregor Blaise
Kirsty Armstrong	Emma Bayliss	Tom Boardman
Paul Askew	Cameron Bell	Ben & Kellie Booth
Archie Austen	David A Bell	Pam & Ted Borman
Ross Baillie	Sir Les Bell	Karl Bovenizer

Chris Brace

Elizabeth Bray

Jay Bray

John J Bray

Katie Bray

Laura Bray

Sara Bray

Suzanna Bray

Kari Bray-Kelly

Bill Breckon

Christian Brett

Adam Broadway

Graeme Broom

Malcolm Broom

James Brown

Martin Bryson

Aedan Andrejus Burt

Tim Butler

Kathleen Callahan

Malia Camens

Alia & Luke
    Campbell-Crawford

Jon Cannon

Peter Cansell

Xander Cansell

Maggot
    CaptainOfVice

Kate Carter

Castle Mews Girls

Andrew Catlin

Roger Cavanagh

Sarah Chalmers Page

Chee-Lan Chan

Jill Chase

Arshad Chowdhury

Anan Christie

Neil Christie

Mr & Mrs TJ Clark

Ric Clark

Terry & Kate Clark

Clark Foyster Wines

Amy Cleary

Emma Cohen

Simon Cohen

Robbie Collin

Dan Collins

Peter Alan Connelly

Andy Cook

Angus Cook

Del Cook

Nick & Jill Cook

Richard Cook

Theo Cook

Paul Cooper

Paul 'Coops' Cooper

Nancy Corbett

Bernadette Costello

Hugh Costello

Charlotte Cotterill

Countessa of
    Beachy Head

Buzz Cousins

Andrew Cox and
    Christina Moschou

James Crawford

John Crawford

Peter Crawford

Alastair Cross

Robbie Cunningham

Valerie Daly

Michael Darby

Ben Davidson

Robin Davis

Tarquin de Burgh

Graham Deas

JF Derry

Michael DiCarlo

Brian Digby

Ivan Dixon

Michael Driver

Robert & Sarah Duncan

Joseph Durrant

Robert Eardley

Charles Egan

Carl Emery

Gerald Epstein

Derek Erb

Bernard Fassone

Harriet Feeny

John Ferry

Hannah Fleming

PJ Fleming

Ben Fletcher-Watson

Sue Fletcher-Watson   Karen Harrison   Jane Tennyson Lee
George Flickinger   Luke Harrison   Robert Lee
Chris Ford   Maree Harrison   Nick Leffler
Ilana Fox   Caitlin Harvey   Beth Lewis
Ross & Katrina Frame   Cynthia Hayward   Paul Lewis
Isobel Frankish   Cynthia Brian Hayward   Peter Linacre
Ian Furbank   James Hedges   Andy Lipscombe
Anthony Fusaro   Todd Heiler   Alisdair Lynch
Emilianna Fusaro   E O Higgins   Johnny Lynch
Mark Gamble   Stephen Higgs   Lillian McCaw
Philippe Gard   Becca & Matt Hopkins   Christina McComb
AC Gaughen   Joseph Howley   Jane McCulloch
Phil Geraghty   T. C. Hudson   Daniel McCurdy
Jason Gibb   John Humphrey   Archie Magnus
Jo Gibson   Michael Husbands   Mcdiarmid
Anna Gierth   Julian Hynd   Elspeth McDiarmid
Jane Gilchrist   Lois Ireson   Sarah McDiarmid
Alexander Glonek   Fiona Jeaffreson   The McDiarmid Clan
David Graham   Jess Jethwa   Patricia McEvoy
Charlotte Gray   Anne Jones   Mo McFarland
Dana Green   David Jones   Peter Macfarlane
Robert Greybrook   Eve Keighley   Robert McIntosh
Julien Grill   Conor Kelly   James McIntyre
William Hackett-Jones   Oisín Kelly   Gemma McKenzie
Simon Hamlet   Sam Kenchington   Andrew Mackie
Tom Hands   Dan Kieran   Fiona Mackintosh
Alistair Hankin   Kevin Kieran   Kirsten Mackintosh
Maria Hansen   Louise Knowles   Ben McLeod
Rueben J. Hansen   Kevin Kodama   Mark McLeod
Craig Harper   Alastair Lawrie   Andrew McNeill
Elysia Harrison   Jimmy Leach   Juel Mahoney

David Manson
Rupert Markland
Orlando Mason
Ashika Mathews
Catherine Matthews
Jules Maury
Matthew Mawtus
Bryan Melville
Eva Menuhin
Deborah Metters
Tony Milanowski
Creampuff "Casper"
  Milktoast
Craig Millar
Nikola Miller
John Mitchinson
Thibault Molcard
Jim Mooney
Jesus & Jenni
  Moorhouse
Kate Morrison
Trevor Morrison
Ben Murray
Gus Murray-Smith
Bill Nanson
Walter Neilson
John Nelson
Andrew Nielsen
Ross Nutter
Evert Oosthoek
Monique Outteridge

Ned Palmer
Nick Parfitt
Magnus Paterson
Sarah Patmore
Tony Pekarik
Kevin Percival
Anna Pettersson
Justin Pollard
Christopher Potter
Luke Potter
Marcus Potter
Ceri Putman
Yasmina Rahiman
Freya Reinsch
Emma Rettie
Louise Rice
Eric Roberts
James Robertson
Giles Roff
Alicia Romano
Mark Rushworth
Christoph Sander
Joanne Sayer
Trevor Schoenfeld
Scott Dunn Travel
Dick Selwood
Tom Sermon
D & E Skeels
Catherine Slater
Ali Slaughter
Andy Smith

Guy Solan
Lisa Somerville
Jenny Southee
Matthew Spicer
Richard Spiers
Sam Sprot
St. Andrews Wine
  Company
Bridget Stahl
Megan Stahl
Amy Stewart
George Stewart
James Stewart
Caroline Stirling
Lewis Stowe
Simon Stoye
Cosmo Sutherland
Karen Tait
Mark Tait
Stephen Taylor
Jo Tennant
Sarah Thelwall
Ian Thompson-Corr
Ian Tierney
Sarah Tierney
Victoria Timberlake
David Toogood
David Tubby
Ian Turnbull
Mi Van de Water
Mark Vent

Rupert Walker
Roger Wall
Alice and Trevor
   Wallace
Ted Walsh
Joe Walton
Miranda Ward
Eddie Warke
Harry Watkins
Dave & Emma Weale

Peter Webb
Nomar Weinleffe
Chandler K. Wells
Johnny Wender
Dara Weston
Jamie Wightman
Roger Wightman
Adam Wilkinson
Bill Williams
Eliot Wilson

Swig Wines
A Wisbey
L Wisbey
Peter Wood
Daniel Wright
Natalie Yates
Clarisse Zalcman
Daniel Zalcman
Christopher Zegel
Monique Ziervogel

A NOTE ABOUT THE TYPEFACES

The main typeface used in this book is Electra, designed in 1935 by American designer D.W. Dwiggins. He is credited with coining the term 'graphic designer', and made significant improvements in book design during his tenure with Alfred A. Knopf publishers. Dwiggins, a son of Martinsville, Ohio, moved to the Boston area in 1904, taking up a position at the invitation of America's greatest typographer, Frederick Goudy. After moving he quickly became a Boston Red Sox fan, a love affair that lasted over 50 years until his death in 1956. The Dwiggins archive, including the original drawings for his Electra typeface, is held at the Boston Public Library.

The titling font is Roma. Released in 2011 by the Canada Type foundry, the face was designed by Tom Lincoln, a fan of the minor league Eugene Emeralds. The 'inscribed' weight of the typeface is displayed on the title page.